D0435366

YOU ARE THE TARGET

• *Big Tobacco: Lies, Scams – Now The Truth* •

Georgina Lovell

Copyright © 2002 Georgina Lovell

The views and opinions expressed in this book
You Are The Target
Big Tobacco: Lies, Scams – Now The Truth
are those of the author Georgina Lovell
who is solely responsible for its content.

Cover and printing by Ticky Graphics & Printing

Cover photographs credit Mark Brennan Photography,
Vancouver, B.C.
and include donations from personal archives

Acknowledgement to Thelma Barer-Stein for invaluable
assistance in producing this book and suggesting the title.

All rights reserved, including the right to reproduce this work in any
form whatsoever, without permission in writing from the author,
except for a few brief passages in a review.

If you are unable to order this book from your local bookseller, you
may order directly from the publisher. Quantity discounts available
to schools and smoking cessation programs.

Published by Chryan Communications, Vancouver
British Columbia, Canada

Contact us for orders and information:
Phone: (604) 740-3883
Fax: (604) 740-3884

Email: chryancomm@dccnet.com

Website: www.you-are-the-target.com

ISBN 0 - 9 7 3 0 6 7 0 - 0 - 4

Printed in Canada

• FOREWORD •

It's truly a David and Goliath venture, and about time, too! From the opening paragraph, the first chapter of your book makes it obvious you aren't about to pull any punches in your fight to reveal the cynical deceit of the tobacco industry. It's outrageous, infuriating and entertaining.

On September 11, 2001 terrorists murdered 6,000 people and the world mobilized in order to prevent it ever happening again. Yet the tobacco industry kills that many people every week in North America alone, but their powerful ploys of mass psychological manipulation somehow keep us from reacting.

Your book is just the medicine. It is passionate, articulate and readable. Through irony, intense indignity and obviously passionate caring for humanity you reawaken my desensitized emotions. Not a small task.

As a medical educator whose life is dedicated to prevention of morbidity and mortality from addictive disorders, I am delighted to throw my full support behind this important and very classy book.

Ray Baker,   M.D., F.C.F.P., F.A.S.A.M.
Assistant Clinical Professor,
University of British Columbia Faculty of Medicine
Health Quest Occupational Health Corp.

• DEDICATION •

The impetus for this book came from two remarkable people: my parents.

They met at school in Basingstoke, U.K. when they were both 14.

My father was very English: tall, handsome, a pianist, a broad-shouldered oarsman, skier, yachtsman and tennis player, successful in business and great fun. He died, miserably, of small cell lung cancer as the result of a lifetime of cigarette smoking - sworn under oath by one tobacco executive to be no more addictive than gummi bears candy. (1)

My mother liked Canada so much she stayed following a holiday to visit relatives. A love story unfolded when my father followed her across the Atlantic, and she married him the same afternoon his ship docked at Montreal on a sunny autumn day in 1937. She lived with him and loved him for the next half century. A former beauty queen, London fashion model, gold medal track star and skier, she now requires the use of an assisted breathing machine at four-hour intervals, and supplemental oxygen through a plastic tube up her nose twenty-four hours a day because she has emphysema. Her lungs are ruined from 50 years of exposure to cigarette smoke - publicly proclaimed by a tobacco research scientist as no more harmful than applesauce. (2)

I hope with all my heart anyone who has fallen prey to tobacco will find within these pages the resolve they need to become tobacco free forever.

• INTRODUCTION •

This book will be of interest to anyone in the world who has been personally involved in some manner with tobacco and/or unwilling exposure to tobacco smoke. This book will be of interest to anyone who has seen a loved one ravaged by the consequences of smoking, is or has been engaged in a personal battle to overcome their own nicotine addiction; anyone whose evening out has been ruined by unwilling exposure to others' tobacco smoke; anyone who has found it necessary to fumigate their clothing after a party; anyone who sees the outrage of any condition of employment requiring exposure to the toxic waste produced by cigarettes, pipes, and cigars. In other words, this book will be of interest to everyone.

As an unwilling young passenger in a smoke-filled family car, I regularly became "car sick" as a child. My childhood ear infections, asthma attacks and three-times-a-year bouts with tonsillitis resulted from living in the house of a smoker who believed the 1950's and 60's tobacco propaganda about smoking being good for you (menthols especially, for sore throats, so they said). Cigarettes claimed the lives of my father and my father-in-law. My mother and my mother-in-law lived all their married lives with smokers, and their health seriously suffered because of it.

In accordance with the tobacco cartel's agenda, I began smoking at the age of 16 when my father gave me my first cigarette, as I worried over final exams. I remember the occasion well. I coughed and felt dizzy but after persevering managed to puff away and look (or so I thought at the time) very adult and out-of-the-fridge cool. At college I listened to Joan Baez and Bob Dylan and Gordon Lightfoot. I wore baggy black turtleneck sweaters and tight jeans and white lipstick and wrote angst-filled poetry into the night. Stick insect-thin, I believed a lighted tube dangling from my pale lips contributed an aura of mystery and the desired image of a mind too immersed in existential thought to worry about anything as mundane as the health consequences of what, all my life, I'd seen my robust father doing. From the moment he woke up until the moment he fell asleep he smoked, and sometimes he even awoke during the night in nicotine withdrawal. He was a wonderful father and a more than adequate provider. I wanted for nothing. No big deal that he smoked - at least, that's what tobacco said in their advertisements. In the 1950's and 60's, nobody doubted what tobacco advertisements said.

Fortunately I grew up, and in my mid-twenties when the time arrived to consider motherhood, I decided my babies would not be nicotine babies. I went through maybe one or two packs of cigarettes a week, mostly on weekends at parties. I never smoked at home, because my husband objected. I decided to wait until I had gone one month without a cigarette to tell him I had quit, and when I did, his response came as a shock.

"I know", he said. He told me the stench of stale smoke no longer walked through the door with me, and he had known from the first day how long it had been since my last nicotine fix.

Many years later, on an idle summer evening in 1998, I introduced myself to the internet. Fascinated by the resources available in the comfort of my own home I surfed and crashed and generally acquainted myself with cyberspace and all it offered. One of the sites I stumbled upon at CNN called itself A Message Board, and the topic being discussed, allegedly civilly, was smoking. I prefer to call it a *bored*, because it's where I went, when I was.

I stated what I considered a friendly and open minded opinion supporting restriction of involuntary exposure to secondhand smoke. Within hours the personal insults and attacks against me started. The first, predictably, called me a "nico nazi". "Nico nazi", and "health nazi" are the terms invented by Victor L. Crawford when he worked as a paid tobacco lobbyist. (A smoker, he later succumbed to throat cancer and with a cancer-riddled voice, spoke out loudly against the tobacco cartel who had once paid him to think up phrases like "health nazi".) "Nico nazi", like all tobacco propaganda, became a well-used invective, liberally used as an emotive counter challenge to label those who make smoke-free choices as control-freak, goose-stepping partypoopers. Regularly invoked by tobacco front groups, this term guarantees controversy and maintains the illusion of violation of personal rights and freedoms when smokers cannot smoke in public (conveniently overlooking, every time, the rights of the smoke-free not to smoke).

My interest piqued and each challenge sent me researching tobacco issues, on and offline. Tobacco apologists sound so convincing sometimes it almost appears necessary to re-check the facts. I became the "anti" a small handful of tantrumming tobacco supporters grew to love to hate. An "anti" is tobaccospeak for anyone who supports smoking restrictions, and is one of the few repeatable abuses levelled against me. An "anti" can also be labelled a "nico nazi"; in fact, the two are virtually inseparable when tobacco front groups describe anyone who supports the rights of the smoke-free. I have been stalked via the internet, and regular attempts have been made to discover personal details about myself and my family. I have received threats of vandalism to my home. Think of the filthiest names you have ever heard and I have been called all of them (yes, even that one). I also received a not-so-subtle death threat on an open internet board, and the police now have a file on the individual who committed this cowardly act of desperation and rage. A major publishing house wrote to me personally to suggest I abandon this "book idea" (tobacco tentacles reach far). My family, my city, country, nationality, hobbies and even my dogs have been denigrated, viciously insulted and verbally attacked by pro tobacco people – some of whom I now know are planted by the tobacco cartel to work these message boards and flood them out of existence with nonsense posts when there is no hope of recovering lost arguments defending the indefensible use of tobacco.

The reason for all the meanspirited aggression directed my way? I support restrictions on the sale and consumption of tobacco, consistent with those imposed on alcohol. I advocate full disclosure of additives and ingredients in tobacco products, and clear warnings about the health consequences of tobacco use, consistent with readily accepted consumer standards applying to a tube of toothpaste or a bottle of over-the-counter cough syrup.

I have always believed offensive and aggressive people are the best teachers of all. None better exist anywhere, than the pro tobaccies who stalk internet message boards, especially the unmoderated forums where strangers say with complete impunity anything they can manage to type on a screen. Being courteous to decently-behaved people presents no challenge at all. Remaining civil in the face of unrelenting, unwarranted profane personal attacks provided unique lessons in patience and tolerance for others' right to free speech, even when the courtesy is not reciprocated. Without predictable tobacco propaganda soundbytes I would never have completed the research I did which led me to the writing of this book. What I have to report about nicotine addiction and the tobacco cartel remains accurate, intact, and well supported. I am not the source of information, but the vehicle for presenting it to you. I am not the one who claims 90% of lung cancer occurs in smokers and ex-smokers; the Harvard School of Medicine say that. I'm just passing information along previously known mostly by medical professionals - and, of course, the tobacco industry.

If tobacco representatives remain consistent with their actions on internet message boards, I may well become a real-life target. When irrefutable information contrary to tobacco interests continues to be presented, the strategy has been to intimidate, threaten and attempt to personally defame anyone who speaks out about tobacco's shameful history of deception and greed, and their multibillion dollar annual profits made from their products which cause addiction and suffering.

The tobacco cartel use you, and me, and everyone you know and don't know, as target practice for what they claim is their legal right to market a legal product. They tell you nicotine addiction and using their products are "adult choices" - can you think of a better way to encourage a 13-year old to try anything, than to tell them that? Informed choice requires *all* the information, not just what you see in glossy cigar ads and tobacco supported Hollywood movie stars. When you've read the rest of the information contained in the following pages, I hope you're in a more informed position to decide whether you want to comply with the plans the tobacco cartel have for you.

Or not.

• CONTENTS •

Glossary of Tobacco Terminology

BATCO: British American Tobacco Company

B & W: Brown & Williamson Tobacco Corporation

Bates Numbers: Bates numbers are the unique identifying numbers assigned to each page of each court document, now a matter of public record. The tobacco cartel must post their original secret documents on the internet. No specifications exist in the directive to make them easily accessible, however. Paul Billings of the American Lung Association said "There does not appear to be any way to short-cut and search for specific documents. They are still secret. They are hiding in plain sight."

Cigarette Papers: On May 12, 1994, a package containing 4,000 pages of confidential internal tobacco industry documents was delivered anonymously to the office of Professor Stanton Glantz at the University of California, San Francisco. These documents contain the dirty secrets about Brown & Williamson covert activities, and its multinational parent, British American Tobacco for over than thirty years.

CIF:
Centre for Individual Freedom, tobacco industry front group.

CTR: Council for Tobacco Research, tobacco-fronted and tobacco-funded.

ETS: Environmental Tobacco Smoke. This is the tobacco-created euphemism for secondhand smoke.

FDA: Food & Drug Administration (U.S.)

FTC: Federal Trade Commission (U.S.)

Liggett Tobacco: Liggett Group Tobacco

Lorillard: Lorillard Tobacco Company

MSA: Master Settlement Agreement. On November 23, 1998, attorneys general representing 46 states, the District of Columbia, and the five U.S. territories signed an agreement with the major cigarette companies to settle all the state lawsuits seeking to recover the Medicaid costs of treating smokers. The Master Settlement Agreement contractually imposes some restrictions on tobacco advertising, marketing, and promotion and requires the manufacturers to make annual payments totalling over $245 billion.

NSA: National Smokers' Alliance front group set up by Philip Morris

PM: Philip Morris Tobacco

RJR: R.J. Reynolds Tobacco Company who own RJR Nabisco Foods

SHS: Secondhand smoke. Secondhand smoke has two sources: mainstream smoke emitted from the lighted and unfiltered end of a cigarette and sidestream smoke, the smoke exhaled by smokers.

TASSC:
The Advancement of Sound Science Coalition, Tobacco front group formed by Philip Morris in 1993. Disappeared in 1998 following exposé in New York Times.

TE: Numbered documents entered as Trial Exhibits

TIMN: Tobacco Institute documents

WHO: World Health Organization (called World Health Oppression by tobacco front groups)

• GENESIS •

A Chronology of the Marketing of Nicotine Addiction

"We now possess a knowledge of nicotine far more extensive than exists in published scientific literature." *(February 13, 1962 BATCO Report, "The Effects of Smoking, Trial Exhibit 11938)*

Historically the earliest association ever made with tobacco use as we know it today has been Sir Walter Raleigh. In July 1586 he returned to England with the first shipment of tobacco from Virginia, dried and crushed and smoked in pipes. Just under one hundred years earlier, however, Christopher Columbus had accepted gifts of fruit, spears, and fragrant dried tobacco leaves from the Arawacks in San Salvador. Columbus and his men copied the Arawack custom of rolling dried tobacco in palm or maize leaves and lighting one end to enable inhalation of tobacco smoke from the unlighted end. Rodrigo de Jerez, a Spanish sailor, can claim to be the first European smoker. When he returned to Spain with his newly acquired hobby of "drinking" smoke from the unlighted end of rolled tobacco leaves, the smoke issuing forth from his nostrils alarmed the townspeople sufficiently to cause his imprisonment for demonic behavior during the Spanish Inquisition. Seven years later upon his release, the smoking fad had taken hold and become accepted.

Tobacco is the common name of the plant *Nicotiana tabacum* and to a limited extent *Nicotiana rustica.* The common name was derived from *tabaco*, meaning a roll of tobacco leaves, or the tube or pipe in which the Indians or Caribbees smoked this plant. Some consider the word derives from *Tabaco*, a province of Yucatan, where Spaniards claimed its discovery; others claim it is named after the island of Tobago, one of the Caribbees. Tobacco is also processed for chewing and snuffing (drawing up powdered tobacco into the nostrils by directly inhaling).

American Indians believed tobacco contained medicinal qualities and used it extensively in ceremonial rituals such as the smoking of the peace pipe. Natives of both North and South America developed early tobacco culture and its introduction to the rest of the world started with a European debut in the l6th century. The *Nicotiana* plant derived its name from Jean Nicot, the French Ambassador to Lisbon. He sent the first European tobacco seeds to Catherin de Medicis, Queen of France, to treat her migraines. Portugese and Spanish sailors transported tobacco from Europe to far-reaching destinations they travelled.

Minimal records exist about early tobacco culture outside Europe. Some dates of interest include Santa Domingo, 1531; Cuba 1580; Brazil 1600; Jamestown, Virginia 1612; Maryland, 1631. Tobacco became a literal cash crop in exchange for European manufactured commodities.

Following the American Revolution, tobacco growing expanded from Virginia and Maryland into Kentucky, Tennessee, North Carolina, Ohio and Missouri. Fire curing dried tobacco leaves enabled this cargo to sustain long ocean voyages to Europe.

Tobacco has provided significant revenue in many countries of the world, from taxes on the stored leaf and on manufactured products, from duties on imports (as in the United Kingdom) and profits from the operation on government monopolies existing in many European countries and Japan, where revenues collected on tobacco products - specifically cigarettes – exceeds the sale value received by farmers for the crop.

King James I of England issued the first official health warning for tobacco and could claim to be the first "anti" in recorded history. His famous quote survived nearly 400 years, when he said:

"Smoking is a custome lothsome to the EYE, hatefull to the NOSE, harmfull to the BRAINE, daungerous to the LUNGS, and in the black stinking fume thereof, neerest resembling the horrible Stigian smoke of the pit that is bottomlesse". (1)

Unfortunately he was partly mistaken when he predicted tobacco would be a "filthie noveltie". Filthy, yes – from day one. However, it would be four hundred years for the "noveltie" to wear thin and serious questions arise about the consequences of tobacco use.

Health authorities maintained interest in the consequences of smoking, although no formal indictment of tobacco use happened until 1966 when the tobacco industry lost the long fight to keep the connection of negative health consequences separate from any association with use of their products. In 1954 the American Cancer Society and the British Medical Research Council reported independently, following separate three year research projects, that smokers had higher death rates than non smokers.

In 1962 the Royal College of Physicians of London, England summarized the evidence on tobacco-caused disease and declared cigarette smoking to be a serious health hazard. In 1963 a second American Cancer Society report provided evidence that death rate for cigarette smokers increases in direct proportion to the amount smoked. In January 1964, an advisory committee appointed by the U.S. Surgeon General ended a two-year study with the conclusion that cigarette smoking was associated with the 70% increase in lung cancer death rates for American males for the decade between 1950 and 1960. The report concluded that cigarette smoking was not only associated with lung cancer, but also coronary artery disease, chronic bronchitis and emphysema. The report addressed pipe smoking and concluded it is linked with lip cancer.

"The cigarette should not be construed as a product but a package. The product is nicotine. Think of a puff of smoke as the vehicle for nicotine." (*William L. Dunn Jr., Philip Morris researcher, after taking part in a 1972 Caribbean meeting held by the Council for Tobacco Research*)

In 1965 federal legislation was passed in the U.S. requiring all cigarette packages sold after January 1, 1966 carry health warning labels. Over 50% of all American males smoked at that time. Within three months of the U.S. Surgeon General's report, cigarette sales dropped by 20%, but within a year had returned to a national average of 42.6% of the population who smoked (52.5% for men, 33.9% for women). Smoking rates would not fall significantly for twenty years. In 1985 , 30.1% of the population smoked (32.6% men, 27.9% women) (2)   In the year 2000, 25% of the general population smoke and the most alarming increase is among teenagers.

A Brief History of Tobacco Trivia

> **600-1000 AD** First pictorial record of tobacco being smoked found on Guatemalan pottery
> **1492** Columbus discovers tobacco in the New World. He is offered "certain dried leaves" which, he records in his journal, "gave off a distinct fragrance".
> **1620** 40,000 lbs. of tobacco imported to England from Virginia.

> **1632** Massachusetts prohibits public smoking.
> **1660** The court of Charles II returns to London from exile in Paris, bringing the French court's snuffing practice with them; snuff becomes an aristocratic form of tobacco use.
> **1670** The Berne, Switzerland town council establishes a special Chambres de Tabac to deal with smokers, who face the same penalties as adulterers.
> **1760** P. Lorillard established the first tobacco manufacturing company in New York
> **1794** U.S. Congress passed the nation's first law on tobacco taxes.
> **1847** Philip Morris opened a shop in England selling hand-rolled Turkish cigars.
> **1849** John E. Liggett opened a tobacco establishment in St. Louis, Missouri.
> **1858** Robert Morris and his son establish the first tobacco factory in Durham, North Carolina, manufacturing "Best Flavored Smoking Tobacco" for pipes.
> **1874** Washington Duke builds his first tobacco factory.
> **1875** R.J. Reynolds opens a company to produce chewing tobacco.
> **1876** Benson & Hedges receives a Royal Warrant from Edward VII, Prince of Wales.
> **1877** J.E. Liggett & Brother incorporates as Liggett & Myers Company.
> **1890** The Duke family establishes the American Tobacco Company.
> **1894** Brown & Williamson form a partnership in Winston-Salem, making mostly plug, snuff and pipe tobacco products.
> **1899** The R.J. Reynolds Tobacco Company incorporates.
> **1900** British tobacco companies join to form the Imperial Tobacco Group.
> **1901** Buchanan "Buck" Duke unites Continental and American Tobacco companies to form the Consolidated Tobacco Company.
> **1901** BATCO (British American Tobacco Company) is formed.
> **1901** Philip Morris comes to the U.S. to sell cigarettes.
> **1904** Duke combines all his tobacco holdings in the American Tobacco Company.
> **1907** U.S. Justice Department files anti-trust charges against the American Tobacco Company.
> **1911** American Tobacco Company dissolved in anti-trust action.

➤ **1912** R.J. Reynolds produces *CAMEL* cigarettes, considered to be the prototype for modern cigarettes as they are known today.

➤ **1913** U.S. Lung Cancer rate is 0.6 per 100,000 (U.S. Census Bureau) 371 reported cases reported for the year.

➤ **1918** The generation of soldiers returning from WWI are addicted to nicotine. Those opposed to free cigarettes for soldiers are called traitors.

➤ **1925** Lung cancer rate is 1.7 per 100,000 (U.S. Census Bureau).

➤ **1926** Lloyd (Spud) Hughes sells his menthol recipe for Spud cigarettes to Axton- Fisher Tobacco Co., which markets mentholated cigarettes nationally.

➤ **1927** BATCO acquire Brown & Williamson.

➤ **1930** 2,357 cases of lung cancer reported in the U.S.

➤ **1931** First filter-tip cigarette manufactured, "Parliament".

➤ **1932** Brown & Williamson introduce "Kool" in competition with Axton-Fisher's "Spud"

➤ **1940** 7,121 cases of lung cancer reported in the U.S. (U.S. Census Bureau).

➤ **1945** President Roosevelt designates tobacco as a protected crop. Cigarettes are included in soldiers' C-Rations. By the end of WWII cigarette sales peak at an all-time high.

➤ **1948** Lung cancer has grown five times faster than other cancers since 1938.

➤ **1951** Union at R.J. Reynolds is de-certified for "red-baiting"

➤ **1956** R.J. Reynolds introduces "Salem", their first filter-tipped menthol cigarette

➤ **1968** Philip Morris introduces "Virginia Slims" aimed at attracting female smokers, advertised with a Women's Lib theme. By 1985 lung cancer surpasses breast cancer as the number one killer of women.

➤ **1969** Congress passes The Cigarette Act of 1969, banning all advertising on radio and television

➤ **1972** Arizona passes the first comprehensive law protecting non-smokers from secondhand smoke

➤ **1983** San Francisco voters use a referendum to foil the tobacco industry's attempt to repeal workplace smoking ordinance

➤ **1985** Philip Morris buys General Foods. R.J.Reynolds buys Nabisco (RJR Nabisco)

➤ **1988** Smoking banned on all U.S. domestic flights of less than two hours.

- ➤ **1990** Smoking is banned on all interstate buses and all domestic airline flights lasting six hours or less
- ➤ **1991** First local ordinance restricting tobacco billboards passed in Long Beach, California
- ➤ **1998** Congressman Waxman releases documents from R.J. Reynolds Tobacco Company for the past 30 years, showing that the company's marketing had deliberately targeted youth, ethnic minorities and women.
- ➤ **2001** Lung cancer is the leading cause of cancer death among men and women in the US, accounting for approximately 167,000 deaths each year (99,000 deaths in men and 68,000 deaths in women). 90% of lung cancer occurs in people who smoke or who have smoked. (2)

Tobacco Advertising (3)

1914
The first national advertising campaign was launched of the kind we now recognize. CAMEL cigarettes, with "new acid blend of Burley & Turkish" (acid allows deeper inhalation with reduced cough reflex). Slogans included "The Camels are Coming", and "Tomorrow There Will Be More Camels In Town Than Asia and Africa Combined!"
1917
Lucky Strike launched their "It's Toasted" advertising. Although all tobacco is heat processed, Lucky Strike implied theirs was unique. Their claim stated "Everyone knows that heat purifies and so Toasting Removes Irritants!"
1918
Rivalry between Camels and Lucky Strike escalated into smear campaigns. American Tobacco suspected R.J. Reynolds of spreading rumors of leprosy and syphilis among their factory workers, and treating tobacco with saltpetre.
1919
Free cigarettes included in soldiers' C-rations. Cigarettes gained acceptance with soldiers and dispelled the upper-class-twit image previously associated with smoking. Camel cigarettes hold 40% of the market.
1921
"I'd walk a mile" slogan for Camel cigarettes appeared on billboards.
1924
Marlboro cigarettes initiated in a market campaign to the female popu-

lation. Camel promotional budget hits $7 million per year.

1925

Women consume 5% of cigarettes

1926

Chesterfield billboard advertising appears. Picture of a young woman with the caption "Blow Some My Way". Women smoking market consisted of "flappers", free-thinking college students, naughty sophisticates. This type of advertising is the origin of the image perpetuated by the tobacco industry that women who smoke are sexy, "liberated" (no mention of enslavement to nicotine), glamorous and forever youthful (no disclosure of how smoking causes premature wrinkles and aging of the skin).

1927

Lucky Strike launched the first aggressive advertisement campaign directed to attract women smokers. New York Metropolitan Opera stars paid to provide personal endorsements "Throat Protection for Precious Voices" Chesterfield advertising campaign launched, attacking Lucky Strike's "opera" media campaign. Marlboro issues first advertisement aimed at women. 'Mild as May', showing a female hand.

1928

"Not a cough in a carload" slogan by Old Gold cigarettes.

Lucky Strike cigarettes openly target women: "Reach for a Lucky instead of a sweet" which was altered following protests from the confectionary industry to read "Reach for a Lucky instead of a FATTENING sweet". Old Gold counters with "Enjoy both (cigarettes and chocolate)…two fine and healthful treats".

1929

"There's real health in Lucky Strike…[they] steady the nerves…favorites of many famous athletes who must keep fit, testify that Luckies do not harm their wind or physical condition."

"Physicians maintain that Luckies are less irritating!" The American Medical Association protests this study being used as 'real' science.

CAMELS advertised on the back cover of Time magazine, showing an expensively dressed woman shopping in an exclusive store.

Lucky Strike hires A.A. Brill, psychoanalyst. "Cigarettes are symbols of freedom…sublimation of oral eroticism…a cigarette is a phallic symbol, to be offered by a man to a woman. Every normal man or woman can identify with such a message."

Models hired to smoke and march together in the New York Easter Parade with "torches of liberty".

Lucky Strike uses testimonial of Captain Fried (sea rescue hero and smoker of Old Golds) who credits calm nerves and crew morale to Lucky Strikes cigarettes.

1930

R.J. Reynolds begin radio advertising for CAMEL cigarettes. "Camel Pleasure Hour" and "All Star Radio Review". In an effort to disparage Lucky Strike advertising, RJR spend $300,000 in newspaper advertising "Turning the Light of Truth on False and Misleading Statements in Recent Cigarette Advertising".

1931

Lucky Strike campaign shows pictures of thin smokers with 'fat' superimposed shadows.

Camels introduces 'humidor' packaging with cellophane wrapper. Offers $500,000 (this is during the depression) in prizes receiving an overwhelming response of 952, 229 entries.

Lucky Strike slogan: "Do you inhale? What's there to be afraid of?"

1933

Chesterfield advertises on the back cover of the New York Medical Journal. "Just as pure as the water you drink" and sexually suggestive "They Satisfy". Camel advertising claims "Healthy Nerves".

1934

Camel distributes one million copies of *The Magician's Handy Book of Cigarette Tricks* in a cartoon format. "It's fun to be fooled" also appeared in colored comic sections of newspapers. Camel advertising claims "Get a Lift With Camel".

1935

20% of the female population smoke.

Camel hire Benny Goodman for "Let's Dance" radio show.

Lucky Strike hires Walter Winchell for news broadcasts.

Camel advertising claim "They Don't Get Your Wind".

1936

Chesterfield sign Paul Whitman orchestra for two years on CBS radio.

Camel advertising claims "For Digestion's Sake".

1938

Chesterfield signs Glenn Miller and The Andrews Sisters for radio show.

Camel's advertising claim "Camels Agree With Me".

1940

Magazine advertising for cigarettes appears in ladies' magazines such as *McCalls, Ladies Home Journal, Better Homes and Gardens* and also in *LIFE* and *Time*.

Philip Morris page boy midget "Call for Philip Morris" campaign begins.

1941

Miss America 1941 (Rosemary LaPlanche) endorses Chesterfield cigarettes on billboards, car cards and store displays. Lucky Strike pays copywriter a $10,000 bonus for the sexual implication in the description of their cigarettes as "so round, so firm, so fully packed".

Camels begin advertising in medical journals and set up booths at medical conventions. Models in white lab coats claim that "slow burning produces less nicotine".

1943

"Lucky Strike Green Has Gone To War" connects with a military image. Cigarettes given away, or sold cheaply (3 for the price of 2, etc.) to VA hospitals, soldiers. Package changed from military green to white, following complaints from the ladies that green was ugly and clashed with their dresses.

Philip Morris claims "far less irritating...leading medical experts".

Camel advertisement featured the "T Zone" for "30 day throat test".

The FTC lawsuit launched against R.J. Reynolds for false advertising stated that according to impartial research, smoking Camels did not, as claimed:

1) keep a person in good athletic condition;
2) Camels were not made of more expensive tobacco than in other brands;
3) Camels could not claim the total supply of fine tobaccos produced;
4) Camels did not burn 25% - or any per cent – more slowly than other brands;
5) Camels did not contain 28% - or any per cent – less nicotine than other brands.

Chesterfield uses military images for the advertisements: "Rosie the Riveter" and movie stars in uniform.

1944

Judge rules Old Gold's "like no other" advertising campaign to be "a perversion...using the truth to cause the reader to believe exactly the opposite".

1946

Philip Morris runs ads claiming "an ounce of prevention" with disclaimer that their product has no curative powers.

Chesterfields begins "ABC" campaign (Always Buy Chesterfields).

"More Doctors Smoke Camels" campaign launched.

1947

Camel advertised in New York medical journal in "Experience Is The Best Teacher" campaign in recognition of medical discoverer.

"More Doctors Smoke Camels" campaign continues to run.

1949

Philip Morris campaign claims "leading throat and nose specialists suggest: Change to Philip Morris!"

(Camels never specify who is their "noted throat specialist". Did anyone ask?)

1950's

FTC found Camels at fault (1952) for claims of "aiding digestion", "relieving fatigue", "soothing the nerves". FTC found Camel advertising false and misleading and therefore deceptive". Cease and desist ordered.

FTC investigated Lucky Strike and their claim of preference by "Tobacco Experts 2 to 1", claims regarding less acid, less nicotine, less irritating to throat than other brands. Investigation revealed "experts" were not exclusive Lucky Strike smokers, some were never interviewed, some were completely unfamiliar with grades and qualities contained in this brand – and *50 of 440 "expert testifiers" were not even smokers*. Ordered to cease and desist.

Cease and desist ordered against Old Gold (1952) for their claim that theirs contained less nicotine than other brands. The "difference" amounted to 1/24th of an ounce over twelve months of smoking a pack a day. Fined $40,000.00.

FTC ordered Philip Morris to cease and desist further advertising claims that their product was less irritating to upper respiratory tract because of "moistening". Later dismissed when this ad campaign was abandoned.

FTC ordered Chesterfield to cease and desist (1958) claims that their product would "not harm nose and throat ", was "much milder", because no evidence existed to indicate this was true.

FTC ordered Kool to cease and desist their claim that this menthol brand offered "protection against colds".

In typical tobacco fashion, all these claims were appealed with clever lawyering, to protract proceedings over a period of up to thirteen years, by which time the campaigns were finished, charges dismissed.

Television Advertising had arrived, with sponsorship of prime time shows. Arthur Godfrey and Perry Como were sponsored by Chesterfield; Ed Wynn, by Camel. Old Golds promoted *The Original Amateur Hour* and half of *Stop the Music*. The original *Candid Camera*'s sponsor was Philip Morris and Robert Montgomery hosted *Lucky Strike Theatre*.

Live television perils were well illustrated when Morey Amsterdam had a coughing fit demonstrating how "mild" Chesterfield cigarettes were supposed to be.

Phony smoke rings were dubbed into film, and announcers were encouraged to exhale smoke while talking.

A Lucky Strike auctioneer worked for 5 ½ seconds for a television commercial, during which time he spoke 500-700 words. He hadn't sold tobacco for ten years; worked for 5 ½ seconds and was flown home. Nice work if you can get it!

1952

Old Gold: "For a Treat Instead of a Treatment" "No Other Cigarette Less Irritating…conclusion established evidence by the U.S. Government!"

Chesterfield claims "Nose and Throat Not Affected".

1953

Huge advertising campaign begins for Kent cigarettes with a "micronite" filter. Filter is made of crocidilite asbestos, the most potent carcinogen of the various asbestos filter types. Lorillard tobacco conducted independent testing in 1954, confirming fiber release from their Kent cigarette filters. Lorillard manufactured and sold Kent cigarettes with "micronite filters" made of lethal asbestos, without recall, for another two years. Lorillard sold 13 billion of these cigarettes between 1952 and 1956.

Camels claimed "there must be a reason", although the reason for what remained a mystery.

Chesterfield claimed to be "much milder" but no baseline was provided for comparison.

L & M launch a new brand, calling it "just what the doctor ordered".

American Medical Association drop advertising for alcohol and tobacco products from any of their publications.

Philip Morris launches new campaign for the "cigarette that takes the fear out of smoking" with full credit to a "new ingredient". The mystery ingredient is "D1-G1" – di-ethylene glycol which is more commonly known as anti-freeze. Now offering anti freeze to its customers to set on fire and inhale directly into the lungs, Philip Morris claimed this new and improved product "does not produce irritating vapors present in every other leading cigarette".

1954 - 1956

Tobacco-fronted "Tobacco Industry Research Council" set up, and issued "A Frank Statement to Cigarette Smokers". This attorney-prepared, carefully worded "statement" became the precursor to all future tobacco cartel denials about negative consequences of using their products. It called into question any information suggesting that tobacco consumption causes disease. Tobacco apologists were hatched, and produced predictable tobacco propaganda soundbytes still in use today. When referring to reports from the Surgeon General, the response claimed:

"Medical research of recent years indicates many possible causes of lung cancer. There is no proof that cigarette smoking is one of the causes "(4)

Tobacco marketing began the predictable formula, still in use today, of diluting any negative health consequences of tobacco consumption, and shifting the focus to all the other causes of cancer and ill health. Most importantly, the more serious claims must be prefaced with "we believe", as in:

"We believe the products we make are not injurious to health."(5)

Part two of the Tobacco Formula to divert attention away from how tobacco addicts, sickens and kills its users: Save the most emotive aspect to the end, that of a perceived affront to personal choice.

"For more than 300 years tobacco has given solace, relaxation, and enjoyment to mankind. At one time or another during those years critics have held it responsible for practically every disease of the human body. One by one these charges have been abandoned for lack of evidence."(6)

Viceroy (according to their advertisement) claims its booth was visited by 64,985 doctors at a medical convention. Who's checking?
Kent cigarettes promote their "micronite" filters (made of asbestos)

to be so "safe" they are in use in atomic energy plants, hospital operating rooms and atomic submarines. American Medical Association protests these claims as "outrageous example of commercial exploitation and reprehensible hucksterism".

Consumer Reports discovers that Kent filter tips have loosened, resulting in quadrupled nicotine levels, tars increased by 600%. No public disclosure was made.

Winston sales triple following the grammatically incorrect slogan "Winston Tastes Good Like a Cigarette Should".

Marlboro buys National Football League sponsorship, maintains it for twelve years.

1957

Consumer Reports finds more filters loosened resulting in increased levels of tar and nicotine reaching the smoker. L & M "miracle tip" has 70% more nicotine and 33% more tar than two years earlier.

Kent filtered cigarettes producing more tar and nicotine than Lorillard's unfiltered Old Gold brand. R. J. Reynolds' Winston cigarettes producing more tar and nicotine than unfiltered Camel brand.

July 18-26: Congressional Hearings re "False and Misleading Advertising, Filter Tip Cigarettes"(house report 1372) . Sub-committee gets reorganized into obscurity and non-existence.

Kent's new "micronite" filter results in increased sales from 3.4 billion to 15 billion, rescuing financially distressed Lorillard. "Micronite" filter tips contained crocodilite asbestos, the most potent carcinogen of the various asbestos fiber types responsible for malignant abdominal mesothelioma .

Motivational research makes a debut in creating tobacco advertising.

Market research lists smokers' rationalizations in order of prevalence. (7) Time does not alter some things. The following list of smokers' justifications survives longer than smokers do.

1. I'm OK. No problems yet, so I'm exempt.
1. I just dabble. Only a problem if smokes 2 packs a day.
2. I have to die sometime. Autos are even more dangerous.
3. My doctor didn't tell me to stop. My doctor smokes, etc.
4. I refuse to worry. It's not my nature to worry.
5. I'll take my chances. It hits only a few.
6. I'm young yet. Someday I'll worry about it.

1958

Chesterfield prohibited from further advertising claiming "no adverse affect on nose, throat or accessory organs".

Six companies claim their product has the "lowest tar on the market".

1959

Arthur Godfrey show dropped by Lorillard after Godfrey said smok
ing made him feel bad.

1960

Tobacco industry and the Federal Trade Commission reached a 'voluntary' ban on tar and nicotine claims.

1961 – 1963

Reader's Digest tested filter tips, concluding no improvements had been
made. With no regulations to lower tar and nicotine, no effort was required by the tobacco industry to provide a 'safer' cigarette.

1962 – 1964

A report from the Royal College of Physicians and Surgeons in London,
England prompted a report from the U.S. Surgeon General in January
1964. Both reports concluded that smoking caused lung cancer and probably caused other more common illnesses such as coronary heart disease. The impact on tobacco advertising reached far. Within weeks the
Federal Trade Commission required health warnings on advertisements.
Professional endorsements no longer conformed to the revised advertising standards adopted by the tobacco industry. Per capita cigarette consumption declined 3.5%, but recovered in 1965 and 1966.

1966

Following appeals from the American Cancer Societies and other health
organizations, the FTC reinstated label disclosure of tar and nicotine
levels. Health claims were prohibited.

1970

Congress banned all cigarette advertising on television and radio.

1972

Federal Trade Commission regulation required all cigarette advertisements to carry the same Surgeon General warning that appeared on
cigarette packaging.

1975

Norway impose complete ban on advertising and sponsoring, coupled
with health warnings, public information and age limits on sales.(8)
Long-term reduction of smoking prevalence by 9% (9)

1977

Finland imposes complete ban on advertising, no smoking in public
buildings, age limit on sales, strong public information campaigns.

Reduction of cigarette consumption of 6.7% (10)
1989
Canada imposes complete ban on advertising and sponsoring, with higher tobacco prices.
Corrected for price increases, a long-term reduction of smoking prevalence of 4%. (11)
1990
New Zealand imposes ban on advertising and sponsoring, increases tobacco prices.
Reduction in tobacco sales of 7.5%, of which 5.5% is attributed to ad ban. (12)
1999
New York Times newspaper refuses to accept tobacco advertising. Brown & Williamson spokesman calls this move "pathetic and intellectually weak" and asks "What will they ban next? Fast food because it is high in fat content? Coffee because it has caffeine?". (13) This becomes a mantra for tobacco supporters around the world, with "red meat", "driving cars" and "eating donuts" also classified in the same dangerous category as nicotine addiction, smoking and involuntary exposure to tobacco smoke.
1999
Tobacco billboard advertising banned in the U.S.
2001
Workers Compensation Board in Vancouver, British Columbia (Canadian equivalent to O.S.H.A.) approves amendments to Environmental Tobacco Smoke regulations to further control workers' exposure to second-hand smoke in hospitality, long-term care and provincial correctional facilities. All employers, including those in hospitality, long term care and provincial correctional facilities, must control workers' exposure to secondhand smoke. Reasonable options, such as designated smoking areas or other equally effective means, to protect workers are provided. (14)
2002
British Columbia, Canada Liberal government overrules the Workers Compensation Board smoke-free workplace recommendation to permit smoking in some workplaces (not government offices, however). The B.C. Liberal government admits to receiving campaign funds from the tobacco industry during the 2001 election when they defeated the incumbent N.D.P. party.

• I - WOMEN AND CHILDREN FIRST •
Tobacco Targets the Vulnerable

Addiction preys on the vulnerable. Purveyors of addiction research their market carefully and leave nothing to chance when the potential exists for huge annual profits.

Women – "Project Magic" (1)

Towards the end of the 19th century, the tobacco industry understood the importance of peddling nicotine to women via traditional images of sweet children, fortified with an appeal to the newly emerging suffragette. Even the most coddled of women welcomed the novel opportunity to make their own choices independently of male influence. Inveterate cigarette advertising directed to the untapped female market carried images of a barefoot little girl cuddling a cat, and apple-cheeked babies in prams who declared in cute captions that "PET cigarettes are the best!". Bold new advertising, reflecting newly-found female independence, showed naughty-but-nice young ladies flashing forbidden ankles as they bent over to take a closer look at a package of cigarettes on the ground, the double-entendre caption declaring: "Worth Picking Up!".

Until the years following World War I, only women of loose morals would dare to be seen smoking in public. Tobacco capitalized on the excitement of the forbidden-fruit connection with smoking pitted against traditionally accepted ladylike behavior. This appealing dichotomy has been the foundation for a century to market nicotine to women, particularly young women, with the false claim that only the free-thinking and independent dare to smoke, while thumbing their metaphorical noses at anyone who objects. From the dainty Victorian matron lighting a "Little Darling" cigarette in the privacy of her own parlor, to the party animal 1920's flapper; from WWII Rosie the Riveter, to the 1950's June Cleaver clones; from the bra-burning women's liberationists of the 1960's to the pierced punk rockers of the 1990's - the underlying theme of enticing women to smoke has embraced the fundamental feminine requisites all women share: to make their own decisions – and above all else, do whatever they are convinced is necessary to stay slim.

The counter-image of the smoke-free woman as a puritanical prude whose rejection of nicotine addiction means, as the tobacco ads have said for a hundred years, she loses out in the dating game, doesn't

**Victorian Cigarette Cards –
Notice nobody is actually holding a cigarette**

know how to enjoy herself, and secretly resents her bolder, free-thinking (and, of course, smoking) sisters. This image of the female smoker
continues to be promoted today.

The roaring twenties of post WWI reflected the metamorphosed
woman who had grown weary of artificially laced-up wasp waists and
bustles, elaborate coiffures, ankles tangled in cumbersome yards of vo-
luminous skirts, crinolines and petticoats. Known as The New Generation Woman, the flapper defiantly doffed her corsets, bleached , permed
and bobbed her hair, raised her hemlines scandalously high to the knees
(which any self-respecting flapper curiously rouged and powdered). Fear-
less flappers outrageously plucked their eyebrows, painted their faces
and earned themselves the proud label of "rebel" by the more gentle
generation of their Gibson Girl mothers. A 1922 magazine article describes three stages of flapperdom: the semi-flapper, the flapper and the
super-flapper. The author of one article as it appeared on December 6,
1922 does not take her identity lightly. She tells her parents, "Attainment
of flapperhood is a big and serious undertaking!". (2)

Venturing into previously male-only arenas included cocktails, cars,
crew races – and smoking. Cigarette holders became as mandatory a
fashion accessory for the fashionable flapper as fingerless fishnet gloves,

feather boas and waist-length ropes of pearls. The truly chic cigarette holders collapsed into small pendants worn on a chain around the neck –concealed from the stern eye of strict parents, and available for use as needed. Later model cigarette holders mirrored the long, slim image of the flapper and extended up to 24", often fashioned from mother of pearl or silver filigree to match compacts and lipstick holders. From closet parlor smokers to wild good-time-party-girls in less than a decade, the woman of the 20's caught the attention of the tobacco industry who never fail to recognize a market ripe for the picking.

Underlying this newly found freedom of thought and action remained one of the more pervasive self-imposed conditions of women

What is "convincingly mild"? The cigarettes or her chest?

A slender figure is literally the last thing smokers with lung cancer think about.

through the ages: a slender figure. 1927 Lucky Strikes advertised themselves with the slogan "Reach for a Lucky Instead of a Sweet" with
the clear implication that smoking keeps a woman slim and therefore
attractive to men. Packaged and sold in small satin bags, cigarettes for
the female clientele in the early years of the 20th century were unfiltered and wrapped in gold leaf paper, carefully marketed as small and
dainty, and sometimes perfumed. Brand names appealed to the feminine, sophisticated image tobacco still likes to promote: Little Dar-
lings, Debs Rose Tips, Chic, Duchess, Lady Hamilton, Fems. These
alluring brand names bear little association with the reality of stained
teeth, yellowed fingers, halitosis and smart new hairdos reeking of stale
smoke. Salome brand appealed to the saucy sisters who believed tobacco propaganda reassuring them that the only requirement for in-
stant and irresistible sex appeal could be all theirs – via a tube of dried
tobacco leaves, wrapped in gold metallic paper, set on fire, and placed
dangling from the mouth, while exhaling smoke from the nostrils.

**"Some women would prefer having smaller babies." Joseph
Cullman, CEO, Philip Morris, when asked to comment on the results of a U.K. research project concluding that babies of smoking
mothers are smaller and smoking mothers have more stillbirths
and infant death with 28 days of birth. CBS *Face the Nation*
January 3, 1971 Bates 1005081714/1732**

WWII saw the emergence of an even more independent women than
her 1920's counterpart. With able-bodied men in uniform and away
for many lonely years, women of the 1940's had to assume traditional
"man's work" and proved they could tackle anything - without compromising their traditional roles of wives and mothers. Tobacco advertising adapts to current events, except when sales are adversely affected. The patriotic green "Lucky Strike Has Gone To War" military-
style WWII packaging changed to white following protests from the
ladies who complained the camouflage-green pack clashed with their
dresses. Within six months following the package change from green
to white, Lucky Strike sales increased by 38%. By 1949, 33% of women
smoked, a 500% increase since WWI.

Through the baby-booming 1950's, housewives maintained a status
slightly below sainthood. September, 1940 *Good Housekeeping* magazine published guidelines for Emily Post's "Smoking Etiquette" and

A 1944 advertisement for Old Golds shows a soldier stealing a kiss from a slightly-resisting damsel. It would be positively unpatriotic, *not* to smoke.

Free thinking women in 1949 could still stand by their men - Especially men who are smoking doctors.

these continued into the 1950's, as more women became addicted to nicotine. All conscientious housewives provided cut glass ashtrays for their husbands and visiting guests, and the smartest homes sported decorator coffee-table cigarette boxes made of cut crystal (with matching table lighters), regularly replenished with a fresh guest supply of cigarettes. Gracious hospitality included the offer of cigarettes as much as the offer of food and beverage.

Ever conscious of image, women responded to tobacco industry's guidelines for "Smoking Do's and Don'ts". Correct and incorrect etiquette accompanying the acceptance of a light, nostril exhales and ladylike extinguishing of a cigarette butt were taken very seriously by the 1950's woman. Emily Post remained adamant about acceptable and unacceptable behavior for smokers: it was considered the height of boorishness to light up a cigar or cigarette at a dinner table before the host or hostess did; brides may smoke, but must abstain while wearing their bridal veil (that seems only practical, if not for preservation of healthy lungs, at least for fire prevention). Always, the persistent message relentlessly reminded women they could accept a guarantee that as long as they smoked they would remain forever slim and sophisticated, while their smoke-free sisters (according to the tobacco ads) missed out on all the fun.

The sixties saw the advent of The Pill, increasing divorce rates among those women disillusioned by the artificial happy-housewife role imposed upon them in the 1950's. A new breed of ladies emerged from the 1960's Women's Liberation Movement. Gloria Steinem, Betty Friedan and Helen Gurley Brown wrote books that shocked and shook up established thinking, and they became role models and leaders for cohorts of women who not only publicly burned their bras, but demanded - and got - equal rights in the workplace. A new strain of female rebel had arrived, and the tobacco cartel stayed hot on their heels to sell nicotine addiction through an updated version of The Liberated Woman.

The Virginia Slims advertising hoax of the 1960's and 1970's compared repressed turn of the century women with contemporary images of liberated ladies who enjoyed hard-earned independence and equality with men – which, of course, included nicotine addiction. In 1974, six years after the Virginia Slims 'You've come a long way, baby' campaign, the smoking initiation of twelve-year old girls in the United States had increased by 110%. (3)

From 1991 – 1999, smoking among high school girls increased from 27% to 34.9%. (4) For twenty-five years following the 1960's publication of *The Feminine Mystique* and *Sex and the Single Girl*, the focus of advertising to women increased dramatically to access what tobacco call "market share" of disposable income women had now acquired.

In the early 1990's, as the rate of female smokers continued to increase, the *It's a Woman Thing* campaign arrived on the heels of the *You've Come A Long Way* Virginia Slims scam. Women's independence and self-sufficiency had become established and accepted. The new marketing exploited the in-your-face attitude three generations beyond the giddy good-time-girl flapper who flaunted tradition for fun. The badge of rebellion for the

1968 ad telling smoking women they've "come a long way". Lung cancer in women has more than doubled in the last 20 years. Lung cancer now kills more women than breast cancer.
Truth in advertising: smoking women have come a *very* long way.

Tobacco's Image of Anorexia and Nicotine Addiction for the 1976 Free-Thinking Woman

great-grandmothers of modern women had been shortened skirts and bobbed hair – and, according to tobacco advertisements, smoking. The badge of rebellion for modern women became tattoos and body piercings – and, according to tobacco advertisements, smoking.

Women of the 90's took orders from nobody, with one exception: they still reacted to tobacco's false imagery of slim, chic living made possible only by smoking. Smoke-free sisters were still portrayed as spinsterish, narrow-in-the-nose nannies with no sense of fun. Smoking causes premature wrinkles and aging of the skin, due to years of collagen breakdown resulting in lack of elasticity. However, hundreds of thousands of women bought tobacco's deceptive promise of eternal

Embra. For my woman.

**Embra campaign failed.
The prospect of being owned,
even by a Robert Redford
lookalike, wasn't enough to
sell this brand of nicotine
addiction to the 1970's
woman.**

youth and sophistication, made possible only by nicotine addiction. Correspondingly, women continue to die at record rates of lung cancer.

Martha Byrne, a star of the television soap *As the World Turns*, became the first woman on the Philip Morris *Woman Thing* music label. In 1997 she completed a ten city music tour in the U.S during which free CD's of her recording were given out with each purchase of two packs of Virginia Slims cigarettes. A Philip Morris advertisement referred to her as "daytime Emmy award winner and next big music thing": Martha Byrne, a name to be remembered for being on the lucrative payroll of an industry whose product is twice as dangerous to women than it is to their male counterparts. Lung cancer has surpassed breast cancer as the leading cause of cancer deaths in women since 1987. (5)

Virginia Slims launched an additional *Find Your Voice* campaign, which perpetuated the myth that only nicotine addicted women have the ability to think for themselves. The *Find Your Voice* campaign launched in the late 1990's, met its nemesis - a brave lady who had once been a tobacco model and "Lucky Strike Lady" and "Chesterfield Girl" in the 1950's. Janet Sackman, a smoker and promoter of cigarette smoking for many years, lost her voice box to throat cancer in 1983. In 1990, she was diagnosed with lung cancer and lost one-third of one lung. Following speech therapy and practice in using a mechanical larynx, Janet Sackman addressed the National Press Club on May 24, 2000 to speak out, with the help of an artificial voice box, about the devastating health consequences of smoking which had not caused her to "find her voice", but to lose it.

The National Coalition FOR Women AGAINST Tobacco launched their own campaign against the marketing of tobacco to women via free giveaway cigarettes and a bought-and-paid-for female soap opera starlet. They named their counterattack *Loud and Clear,* and their coalition co-chair , Joanne Koldare, said, "The use of tobacco products continues to pose one of the greatest health threats to women. There are an estimated 23 million women smokers in this country, and we will not let the tobacco industry entice, fool, or seduce more young women with this newest attempt at recruitment." (6)

According to the National Women's Health Information Center, since 1987, lung cancer has been the top cancer killer among American women, with an estimated 66,000 deaths in 1999. Over the past ten years, the mortality rate from lung cancer has declined in men but has continued to rise in women. These alarming trends are under-recognized by women and are due almost exclusively to increased rates of cigarette smoking. (7)

A Philip Morris chief executive agreed to remove the "Find Your Voice" slogan in June 2000 after the Engle trial in Florida when he was asked whether he believed this slogan would be offensive to smokers with throat cancer. Altruism played no part in this decision. Simply, business could suffer should any industry be seen to mock or otherwise draw attention to those whose voices went up in smoke as the direct result of using your products for their sole intended purpose. (8)

"A massive potential market still exists among women and young adults, cigarette industry leaders agreed, acknowledging that recruitment of these millions of prospective smokers comprises the major objective for the immediate future and on a long term basis as well." United States Tobacco Journal, 1950, *Cigarette Executives Expect Added Volume*

Tobacco billboard advertising has become severely restricted in North America and illegal in many places. Increased purchasing power of women becomes the target for tobacco's image of glamor, independence and free-thinking in billboard advertisements elsewhere, such as those seen in Johannesburg, South Africa for Winston Lights. The billboard-high photograph of a well-endowed naked woman about to step out of the shower clearly reveals enticing and glistening wet portions of her body. With a suggestive smile, she enticingly looks into the camera as her hand is teasingly poised to sweep the shower curtain aside. The caption, appearing directly above the cigarette logo for Winston Lights, reads: "Do I look shy?". In another, a petulant sexy blonde sitting on a park bench with a lighted cigarette in her hand looks into the camera and asks "Do I look like I'd cook you breakfast?". The desired bad-girl-in-your-face image perpetuates with another billboard-high image of a black-leather clad biker chick astride a motorcycle asking "Do I look easy to handle?".

The intended tobacco message directed at women for the last century has been clear: smoking cigarettes instantly transforms the plainest and most ordinary woman into an irresistible, glamorous, mysterious and sexy rebel.

Just don't mention the tar-coated lungs.

"Many women are angry by the suggestion of those around them that they should not smoke. For these women, smoking represents an independent and defiant stance. As women are reacting increasingly to restraints put upon them, more women are smoking (of all smokers, 53% are women, 43% are men). However, because of women's nurturing role in society, they are naturally more involved with low tar cigarettes than men (70% of low tar smokers are female)." June, 1985   Philip Morris "Project Magic" Bates Number 2501008130

Cigarettes carrying a "light" or " mild" or "low tar" label typically appeal to the feminine perspective of daintiness. Referring to cigarettes as either "light" or "mild" or "low tar" has been stopped in Canada, following confirmation of the inaccuracy of this claim. The tobacco industry manipulated test results to give false readings of low tar and nicotine content in some brands. Consumers of reduced nicotine brands of cigarettes require a deeper puff for the same nicotine delivery, and consequently develop tumors more deeply situated in the lungs than seen in smokers of "regular" brands. (9)

Women smokers provide fertile pastures for tobacco propaganda. Appealing to their sense of responsibility to their families to take care of their health, while simultaneously promoting the "personal choice" to smoke at all, they were offered the compromise of an allegedly less dangerous "low tar"cigarette. "It is the first cigarette to offer a person the freedom [sic] to choose what strength it shall be." (10)

According to the World Health Organization , 15% of women smoke in industrialized countries, compared with only 8% of women in developing countries. In addition, women in India and Asian countries use chewing tobacco with greater frequency than women in western countries. Current efforts in Vietnam, Korea and India raise the tobacco cartel's hopes of more female nicotine addiction, beginning with addressing the desires of young girls paradoxically concerned about thinking for themselves while conforming to peer pressure – and above all else, staying slim.

It worked once, didn't it?

Cigarette smoking is more deadly for women than for men. Smoking women's risk of lung cancer is double that of her male counterpart. Super model Christy Turlington has been diagnosed with early emphysema while still in her twenties. She had started smoking in her early teens because she believed smoking would keep her slim. Katherine Lauth started smoking in law school, and at age 29 was diagnosed with Stage III tongue cancer. The radiation treatment she endured resulted in limited use of her left arm and slurred speech which is sometimes mistaken for drunkenness. Dina Solloway, model and fashion photographer died of lung cancer from smoking at the age of 28. These brave young women wanted their stories told. These brave young women hope their stories will reach other young women with the clear message, so well stated by a successful trial lawyer and ex-smoker, Katherine Lauth: "My wish is to reach out to other young women who today may feel invulnerable in their youth and beauty. In our society, we see how in the movies and in advertisements, smoking is associated with youth, glamor and beauty. But the truth is, smoking is directly related to an ugly, potentially lethal, and for me, a disfiguring disease. It meant lengthy hospital stays, fear of death, painful procedures, mutilation, nausea, loss of appetite, and the inability to exercise…although I will never be the same person I was before cancer, I am a new person today. I am someone with a disability, a speech impediment, but I am also someone who has found love, someone who is compassionate, loving, dedicated to the law, and someone here to make the world a better place. I am here to stay! " (11)

"Long after the adolescent preoccupation with self-image has subsided, the cigarette will pre-empt even food in time of scarcity on the smokers' priority list." *Smoker Psychology Research* **by Helmut Wakeham, Presented to the PM Board of Directors November 26, 1969. Minnesota Trial Exhibit 10299 Bates # 1000273741**

Tobacco Targets Our Kids

The tobacco cartel have an irrefutable history of lies, fraud, conspiracy and profits über alles. The most despicable aspect of business "ethics" has been their deliberate victimization of children.

The teenage years are the years in which most smokers become addicted to nicotine, when brand selection and loyalty initiates and when conformity to peer pressure is the greatest.(12)   According to tobacco's painstaking market research, only 5% of smokers begin smoking after the age of 24. (13)   Tobacco must recruit 3,000 new smokers *every day* to replace those who quit or die (they are the ones who have quit permanently). It is not surprising to know in a secret 1983 memo summarizing the public-relations initiatives of the Tobacco Institute, Brown & Williamson Tobacco clearly stated they "will not support a youth smoking program which discourages young people from smoking." (14)

Tobacco missed no opportunity to convey their false message that smoking is an enjoyable pastime, reserved only for adults - but children can pretend to be grown-up until they come of age. In 1946, a letter from Brown & Williamson Tobacco to a candy manufacturer gave permission for their brand labels to be copied on packages of candy cigarettes, accompanied by the comment "We have never raised any objection to the use of our labels, feeling (for your more or less private information) that it is not too bad an advertisement". (15)

Spit tobacco (euphemistically labelled "smokeless tobacco", "chew", "dip" and "snuff" by the tobacco industry) involves placing a wad of tobacco between the gums and the cheek and sucking on it. This results in increased saliva production, and spittoons became necessary in public places to discourage disposal of brown spit on public sidewalks and pub floors. Spit tobacco is both highly addictive and a Class A Carcinogen: known to cause cancer in humans.

Skoal Long Cut Cherry spit tobacco looks and tastes like candy. Manufactured in the U.S. by the U.S. Tobacco Company it is meticulously designed to attract a youth market. The cherry flavor is strong and sweet, and lasts two – three minutes, long enough for a child to adjust to the bitter bite of raw tobacco. A former U.S. Tobacco Sales Representative refers to it as "Cherry Skoal is for somebody who likes the taste of candy, if you know what I mean." (16)

The pH level has been exactingly adjusted to slow nicotine absorption for maximum impact on a smaller body while aiding and abetting dependency on this product, aimed for the "pre-smoker" market. Although candy flavored snuff accounts for only 2% of U.S. Tobacco sales, 47% of its total budget is spent promoting this product to young teenagers to prime them for higher impact nicotine delivery devices more commonly known as "cigarettes". (17)

Spit tobacco caused oral cancer and killed Sean Marsee at the age of 18. Spit tobacco caused oral cancer and lost Rick Bender one half of his face at the age of 26. In July 2001, the Bush administration in the United States recently restored the right of the tobacco industry to advertise their products on billboards within 1,000 feet of schools and playgrounds.

"We did not look at the underage market even though I am holding a document in my hand that says we did." (Ex-Phillip Morris President & CEO James Morgan in videotaped testimony in Minnesota St. Paul Pioneer Press, March 3, 1998)

Joe Camel

While publicly denying any direct marketing to underage children, R. J. Reynolds introduced a cartoon character representing its flagship brand whose sales were on its dromedarian knees. Joe Camel epitomized teenage cool, with wraparound sunglasses, leather jackets, white suits a la John "Stayin' Alive" Travolta, racing cars and sailboats – often with at least one beautiful woman in attendance. Entire collections of accessories were spawned, including wristwatches, clocks, t-shirts, flip-flops, baseball hats and even fishing lures. Following the arrival of this camp cartoon character, Camel cigarette sales catapulted from $6 million in 1988 to $476 million in 1991. The tobacco industry reported the brilliant invention of Joe Camel had been directly responsible for this astonishing reversal of fortune. (18)

Joe Camel acquired cult status, especially admired by young teens who aspired to cool-ness via their favourite cartoon character. Camel cigarettes were featured by way of product placement in *Honey, I Shrunk the Kids* and *Who Framed Roger Rabbit?*

California Department of Health Services conducted a survey of 24,000 adults and 5,000 teenagers in 1990 to determine the most recognized brand of cigarettes . Camel and Marlboro were named as the two most heavily advertised brands. When the survey results were analyzed more closely by age groups, less than 10% of those respondents over the age of 45 identified Camels as first on the list of most advertised cigarettes. This percentage more than doubled to 22.7% for the 16 to 17 year olds interviewed. This figure jumped to 34% of the 12 – 13 year olds, who hit the R.J. Reynolds Tobacco bullseye when they identified Camel cigarettes as the most popular brand.(19)

A second study interviewed 5,000 children. Three to six year olds had become as familiar with Joe Camel as they were with Mickey Mouse. (20)

Joe Camel's obituary appeared in 1997 when R.J. Reynolds lost a lawsuit and agreed to not only to remove Joe Camel from their advertising but to pay $10 million for antismoking campaigns in California. Nobody mourned Joe Camel's passing except R.J. Reynolds Tobacco who would have to find a replacement for the increase of $470 million in sales resulting from a jolly cartoon they said was "not directed to children".

R.J. Reynolds would have to think of some other way to maintain the 66% increase in young teenage smokers their old pal Joe had managed to hook.

One of the most positive aspects of tobacco litigation has been the emergence of previously confidential and top secret company documents illustrating for all to see the duplicity upon which the tobacco industry depends to make billions in profit every year. Public statements bear no resemblance to the reality of the business.

One strategy proven to work effectively to educate youth about smoking has been explaining to pre teens and teenagers how they have been singled out by the tobacco cartel as dupes and profit fodder. Teenage rebellion is more effectively directed against the tobacco cartel, instead of deciding to use their products.

And there's more...in the words of those swell tobacco guys who "don't target kids"

"A cigarette for the beginner is a symbolic act. I am no longer my mother's child, I'm tough, I am an adventurer, I'm not square ... As the force from the psychological symbolism subsides, the pharmacological effect takes over to sustain the habit". (31)

"The lower age limit for the profile of young smokers is to remain at 14". (32)

"From a Corporate standpoint, Philip Morris posted a 4 point gain among 14-17 year old smokers". (33)

"Respondents aged 14 to 20 are to used for the cigarette profile report." (34)

"Probability sample of 452 teen-agers ages 12-17" finds that 13 per cent smoke an average of 10.6 cigarettes per day and how the data from the study are consonant [sic] with the findings of other such studies, both at Philip Morris and without." (35)

"We were trying very hard to influence kids who were 14 to start smoking." (36)

FUBYA's

Parents know the best way to encourage a child of any age to do something is to tell them the activity is forbidden and/or reserved for adults only. The tobacco industry takes full advantage of appearing to tell children not to smoke with their "Helping Youth Decide" strategy, while distributing thirteen million school book covers with Philip Morris logo. Thirteen million more remain in storage for future use. (37)

Nobody of any age would be thrilled to learn of how they have succumbed to the deliberate efforts of tobacco to create another generation of dupes – or, as they are known in tobaccospeak, *FUBYAS* (First Usual Brand Younger Adult Smokers) (38).

The "Less Educated Smoker" (39)

Tobacco research confirms an inverse ratio of education and nicotine addiction. Although the better-educated individuals typically begin smoking earlier, they also tend to be the first to quit. (40)

The executive vice-president of a marketing company writes to R.J. Reynolds

"Clearly those people who attended college but have not graduated are the more meaningful target for us." (41)

Public Soundbytes	Private Shame
"Now, I want to be very clear. We do not survey anyone under the age of 18." (21)	"Evidence is now available to indicate that the 14-18 yr. old is an increasing segment of the smoking population. RJR-T must soon establish a successful new brand in this market if our position in the industry is to be maintained long-term." (22)
"If I thought that ad (the Joe Camel campaign) caused any young people to begin smoking, I'd pull it in a heartbeat...it's fun, just like the dog sells Met Life insurance, just like Garfield the cat sells Embassy Suites Hotels." (23)	"They [13 year olds] represent tomorrow's business" (24)
"We do not, under any circumstances, want kids to smoke." (25)	"Realistically if our Company is to survive and prosper over the long term, we must get our share of the youth market. In my opinion, this will require new brands tailored to the youth market."(26)
"We should not be marketing cigarettes to young people. It is certainly anomalous to the Philip Morris I know." (27)	"Marlboro dominates in the 17 and younger category, capturing over 50% of the market." (28)
"What's the tobacco industry doing to discourage youth smoking? A Lot." (29)	"The studies reported on youngsters' motivation for starting ...as well as the starting behavior of children as young as 5 years old." (30)

Project S.C.U.M.

Tobacco research confirms that the nicotine addicted segment of the population will assign the priority of obtaining tobacco products above life necessities such as food and shelter. In the early to mid 1990's, R. J. Reynolds Tobacco decided to increase their sales volume by observing and then closing in for the kill (literally) on distinct minorities in San Francisco. They named this campaign Project S.C.U.M., (sub culture urban marketing), and directed it towards the homeless and gay population who statistically contained a higher than average incidence of smokers. They labelled the target of their attention "rebellious" (there's that word again), "Generation X" -ers, people of "international influence" and "street people". The strategy's goal was to peddle Camel cigarettes from less than traditional retail outlets, or "head shops", and extend a tobacco friendly hand towards the wallets of an already victimized and disadvantaged segment of the population. The San Francisco areas of "Castro" and "Tenderloin" were identified as neighborhoods of particular interest, in handwritten notes in the margin of one of the documents. (42)

Summary

In 1991, Philip Morris conducted a close-up study on women's smoking preferences to monitor the continued success of their sales and promotion of nicotine addiction to the female market. (43)

Tobacco have targeted women for a century, appealing to women's latent sense of rebellion against a world imposing often unattainable expectations of beauty. Tobacco presents itself as the vehicle for transforming Eliza Doolittles into much-admired fair ladies with the flick of a cigarette lighter. Tobacco advertising encouraged women to think for themselves – through smoking, of course – in their Find Your Voice Campaign. This scam backfired horribly when, following surgical removal of her cancerous larynx, a former smoker and cigarette model spoke publicly through her mechanical voice box about the health consequences of tobacco use. Concerted efforts to attract women to nicotine has resulted in a higher incidence of women smokers than ever before. The unique action of female hormones places women at increased vulnerability for smoking related disease. Lung cancer now kills more women than breast cancer.

Hollywood actors disregard their responsibility to their young fans when they accept payment for smoking on camera, clearly displaying cigarette brand logos.

The tobacco industry claim they have never pursued the underage market, a claim proven false with their own research material about candy-flavored tobacco and a smoking cartoon character. Since 1982, the tobacco industry have known that spit tobacco causes oral cancer. (44) Disguising the bitter, foul taste of tobacco with sugary fruit flavors attracts children with the false and misleading implication that "smokeless tobacco" means "safe tobacco". Spit tobacco introduces children to the experience of a nicotine hit with each mouthful, preparing them for smoking, presented as an enticing adult activity.

The time has arrived to pay the tobacco piper. The tobacco-friendly Bush administration has waived previous restrictions preventing tobacco from advertising their products within 1,000 feet of schools and playgrounds.

Higher taxes on tobacco products have a record of reducing consumption, especially among youth. In Canada during the years 1978 – 1991, increases in the taxes resulted in the price of cigarettes increasing by 270%. During this same time, teenage consumption dropped from 44% to 20%.

Three out of four individuals in the western world do not smoke.

Smoking restrictions work to reduce tobacco consumption. They de-normalize smoking and reduce its social acceptance. Ensuing reductions in lung cancer rates follow. In the year 2000, California Dept. of Health Services reported a 14.4% decline in lung cancer rates since the implementation of their restrictive smoking ordinances – compare this with the national reduction of 4% for the same period of time.

Youth smoking cannot be affected without first educating adults to set the best smoke-free examples and not the do-as-I-say-not-as-I-do hypocrisy of too many nicotine addicted adults – who, if they smoke around their children are guilty of child abuse each time they do so. (45)

"A cigarette as a 'drug' administration system for public use has very very significant advantages... All we would want then is a larger bag to carry the money to the bank." BAT Marketing Strategy Document Bates Number 40045998/9956

• II - THEY WILL GO DOWN IN HISTORY •
Tobacco "Saints" and "Ain'ts"

SAINTS

Saint: **A Model of Excellence** (Miriam-Webster Dictionary)

There need be no religious connotation when referring to any individual as saintly. The description of "saint" refers to actions or behavior exceeding any expectation of high standards of morality, and the willing ness to place priority for truth and service above personal comfort.

Wayne McLaren "The Marlboro Man" dies age 53 from lung cancer

"Take care of the children. Tobacco will kill you, and I'm living proof of it." (Wayne McLaren)

Two former Marlboro Men died of lung cancer. One of them, Wayne McLaren, fought hard against the lung cancer that claimed his life at age 53. One notable comment made by this brave man lives on. Before he died he knew he had lung cancer because he had smoked. Fighting to breathe, and terminally ill, Wayne McLaren appeared before the Massachusetts legislature when they were considering a bill to add taxes to cigarettes to pay for health education. He also appeared before a meeting of Philip Morris stockholders, manufacturers of Marlboro and asked them to limit their advertising. While dying a brutal death, he made as many public appearances as he could to warn about the dangers of smoking and apologize for the years he spent working as a model to promote tobacco. His final words for public consumption?

"Smoking caught up with me. I've spent the last month of my life in an incubator and I'm telling you, it's just not worth it."

Philip Morris initially denied that McLaren had ever appeared in Marlboro advertising, but a company spokesperson later conceded that he had appeared in a retail display for Marlboro Texan Poker Cards when presented with photographs of Wayne promoting Marlboro.

R.I.P., Wayne McLaren

"Moreover, nicotine is addictive. We are, then, in the business of selling nicotine, an addictive drug effective in the release of stress mechanisms." July 17, 1963 report by Brown & Williamson general counsel/vice president Addison Yeaman Bates # 2023191002

✳✳

April 14, 1994 House of Representatives Committee on Energy and Commerce Subcommittee on Health and the Environment Hearing on the Regulation of Tobacco Products

MR. CAMPBELL (President of Philip Morris U.S.A.)
under oath: "I believe nicotine is not addictive, yes."
MR. JAMES JOHNSTON (Chairman and CEO of RJ Reynolds Tobacco Company)
under oath: " Mr. Congressman, cigarettes and nicotine clearly do not meet the classic definition of addiction. There is no intoxication."
MR. TADDEO (President of U.S. Tobacco)
under oath: "I don´t believe that nicotine or our products are addictive. "
MR. TISCH (Chairman and CEO of Lorillard Tobacco Company)
under oath: "I believe that nicotine is not addictive. "
MR. HORRIGAN (Chairman and CEO of Liggett Group).
under oath: "I believe that nicotine is not addictive."
MR. SANDEFUR (Chairman and CEO of Brown and Williamson Tobacco Company).
under oath: "I believe that nicotine is not addictive."
MR. DONALD JOHNSTON (President and CEO of American Tobacco Company).
under oath: "And I, too, believe that nicotine is not addictive."

✳✳

Victor Crawford, former tobacco lobbyist, dies of throat cancer March 2, 1996 (age 63)

"I smoked heavily and I started when I was 13 years old. And now in

**my throat and in my lungs, where the smoke used to be, there is a
cancer that I know is killing me. ... Use your brain. Don't let anybody fool you. Don't smoke."** (Victor Crawford, speaking out during
one of President Clinton's live broadcasts from the Oval Office)

A graduate of Georgetown University Law Centre, Victor Crawford
worked as a prominent defense attorney for 30 years before serving for
sixteen years in the Maryland Legislature, first in the House of Delegates and then in the Senate until his retirement in 1983. Victor
Crawford started smoking cigarettes at age 13. By his late thirties his
preference for cigars and pipes prevailed. His fighting spirit found a
focus in lobbying for 'causes', and his expensive taste responded well
to the carrot dangled before him by the Tobacco Institute.

The Tobacco Institute monitored every aspect of every detail about
smoking issues, from laws about vending machines to the latest attempts to enact smoking bans. Victor Crawford instigated many tactics
still in use by pro-tobacco lobbyists, and he coined the phrase "health
nazi" to describe clean indoor air advocates.

In 1990 Takoma Park decided to ban smoking in all its restaurants.
Takoma Park is a city in Montgomery County, 5 miles from the centre
of Washington, D.C. At that time, no other municipality had enacted
total smoking bans, and the Tobacco Institute called in the expertise of
Victor Crawford to defuse the situation. Takoma Park has an Hispanic
population who also have a higher than average rate of smoking. With
the help of computer technology, obtaining a list of all Hispanic-owned
restaurants in the area took minutes to compile and the owner of each
establishment was contacted. Emotive allegations were shouted during an organized demonstration (signs provided) that the proposed
smoking bans were "racist" and "anti-Hispanic" and "unconstitutional".
The proposed bill died.

Victor Crawford learned in 1992 that his sore neck was squamous
cell cancer, described by his doctor as "a textbook case of cancer caused
by smoking". Within a year, new tumors appeared in his lung, liver and
pelvic bone. A coincidental meeting in 1994 between Victor Crawford
and Michael Pertschuk, former Chair of the U.S. Federal Trade Commission and then member of the Advocacy Institute, resulted in a change
of direction for Victor Crawford. He agreed to make available, anonymously, tactics used to fight antismoking efforts. He talked to journalist Roger Rosenblatt, who interviewed Crawford for the New York
Times. He is quoted as saying he decided to speak up, because "if you

stay in the closet, you die in darkness."

His interview appeared in the July 19, 1995 of the Journal of the American Medical Association (1). In it, he revealed the detailed methodology of promoting tobacco. No longer a secret is how the Tobacco Institute exploits the internet and computer technology to obtain, within minutes, smokers' names, addresses, sex, race, and preferred brands. Within twenty-four hours, 500 people can be recruited to attend an organized protest, complete with signs proclaiming any notion of restriction on where smokers may smoke is "un-American", "Hitlerian", "anti-freedom" and "against smokers' rights", etc., etc.

He revealed tobacco's idea of a compromise when ground becomes lost in the defeat of any given clean indoor air bill. When a bill cannot be completely tossed out, work to amend its power until little remains to affect smoking regulations at all, as he did with the Elevator Bill proposed by a Baltimore senator. By the final agreed terms of this bill, a fine for smoking in an elevator would hypothetically be imposed, but only by a uniformed policeman who happened to be in the elevator at the time of the smoking violation. It had become an unenforceable antismoking bill and tobacco claimed another victory.

He revealed that without exception, all successful antismoking efforts begin at a local level, and illustrated why that is the reason tobacco "go crazy" with local antismoking groups. He revealed how easy it is to convince county councils that the issue of smoking bans has nothing to do with health matters but an individual's constitutional rights to whatever lifestyle they choose. With the skill he had acquired in thirty years as a defense attorney, Victor Crawford succeeded in shifting the focus away from the health consequences of exposure to secondhand smoke and into the fiercely protected realm of civil liberties.

The attack-the-messenger tactic has a history of success in diluting what opponents have to say, no matter how true. Dig deep to find dirty linen and if none exists, invent some and feed it to the extensive network of tobacco-friendly media giants.

Before he died, Victor Crawford received an award from the Smoke-Free Maryland Coalition, the first lawmaker of the year award from the American Heart Association Maryland affiliate (named after him, the Victor L. Crawford Lawmaker of the Year Award) and an award from the American Bar Association for his courage in coming forward to tell what he knew.

R.I.P. Victor Crawford.

"I would be more cautious in using the pharmic-medical model – do we really want to tout cigarette as a drug? It is, of course, but there are dangerous F.D.A. implications to having such conceptualization go beyond these walls..." Feb. 19, 1969 Philip Morris memo from William L. Dunn to researcher Dr. Helmut Wakeham. Trial Exhibit 10539

Columnist/Broadcaster John Diamond, 47, Dies of Throat Cancer

"I am the walking, talking - or maybe not talking - equivalent of all those school-day films of blackened lungs and tar-filled test-tubes, the films that never stopped me smoking because the films were about smoking in a different universe - a universe where people got lung cancer and rickety hearts. Everyone I knew smoked; nobody suffered anything worse than weak-mindedness. Good old-fashioned empiricism tells you that you're safe. As it happens, you're wrong, but there's no way I can convince you of it." (John Diamond, *On Smoke and Smoking*, The Times of London, November 8, 1997)

John Diamond began smoking in his teens, right on schedule with tobacco planning. John Diamond did what he did best when he learned in March, 1997 that the lump in his throat was a malignant tumor: with his customary candid humor and wit, he wrote about the frightening and painful journey of a smoker with cancer. Writing about choking on a trachea full of phlegm and the terror of being pinned down for fifteen minutes of radiation treatment would not be comedy fodder for any but the most gifted humorist. Following throat surgery, he described his maimed voice as "Charles Laughton in an underwater version of the Hunchback of Notre Dame". He is the first patient on record at the Royal Marsden Hospital who requested he be allowed to see his own tumor. He described it as roughly the size of a tangerine, "a dark, hard lump with a white, oily centre – the result of years of smoking". Two months after the news that the lump in his neck was malignant, secondary cancer appeared on his tongue.

For a broadcaster married to a master chef, surgical mutilation of his tongue had to be the ultimate in ironic cruelty which he characteristically exploited to keep talking in a different way, without a voice or a tongue. In 1997, he allowed the BBC's *The Inside Story* crew to accompany him and document his experiences and observations as he navigated his way through anxious months of surgery, cancer treatment and waiting. The programme, *Tongue Tied*, aired in 1997, the same year John Diamond won the Columnist of the Year in the What the Papers Say Awards.

From a smoker's point of view, John Diamond communicated the kaleidoscope of emotions and experiences on discovering smoking has caused terminal illness. Through his column in the London Daily Express, he expressed his opinion of the tobacco industry: *Cigarette Firms Want to Stub out the Truth* (January 31, 2001) and *Bid to Cut Cigarette Tax is a Cynical Smokescreen* (February, 2001). Something he said registered sufficiently for David Swan, Chief Executive of the Tobacco Manufacturer's Association to claim John Diamond's accusations abut smuggling were "irresponsible", and respond to the claim about tobacco's promotion of a glamorous smoking image by saying "U.K. Tobacco companies cannot advertise to encourage people to smoke more."

John Diamond's legacy to smokers appears in his autobiography describing the reality of smoking-induced cancer: *C - Cowards Get Cancer, Too – A Hypochondriac Confronts His Nemesis* (2). This book has been proclaimed by cancer patients and oncologists alike as informative, reassuring and real. John Diamond died, age 47, on Friday, March 2, 2001. Another smoking fatality.

R.I.P. John Diamond.

"In the past, we at R & D [research & development] have said that we're not in the cigarette business, we're in the smoke business. It might be more pointed to observe that the cigarette is the vehicle of smoke, smoke is the vehicle of nicotine and nicotine is the agent of a pleasurable body response." Fall, 1969 Philip Morris draft report by William Dunn,, then VP of Research and Development, to the board of directors. *Why One Smokes* Minnesota Trial Exhibit 3681 Bates # 1003287036-48 (This quote is on 1003287837)

Dr. Jeffrey Wigand "The Insider"

I felt that the industry as a whole had defrauded the American public. (Dr. Jeffrey Wigand)

Fortunately not all tobacco "saints" have died painfully and tragically from tobacco use, during their efforts to raise public awareness about the devastating consequences of tobacco use, and the deliberate lies of the tobacco industry. Dr. Wigand obtained his B.A. and Master's Degrees in Organic Chemistry, and Ph.D. in Endocrinology and Biochemistry from the University of Buffalo. An idealistic scientist with a 25-year history of working for healthcare companies (Johnson & Johnson and Pfizer), he joined Brown & Williamson Tobacco on January 3, 1989 as Corporate Vice President of Research and Development, with a full employment package including an annual salary of $300,000+. He would supervise the work of 243 scientists on an annual research budget of $30 million. He believed his mandate to be one of improving the safety of a dangerous product: tobacco. His employer terminated his contract on March 24, 1993. Dr. Wigand had objected to activities he witnessed as necessary to protect profit margins for the tobacco industry.

Dr. Wigand's story begins in Vancouver in 1989, when he represented his employer at a multimillion dollar business conference for tobacco research scientists from Souza Cruz (Brazil), BATCO (U.K.), BAT Cigarettan-Fabriken (Germany), Brown & Williamson (U.S.) and Imperial Tobacco (Canada). They met for four and a half days at the exclusive Pan Pacific Hotel, with an agenda that included how to modify addictiveness of nicotine, how to make secondhand smoke less dangerous to nonsmokers, how to perfect a fire-safe cigarette (one that would not set fire to anything else) and genetic engineering of tobacco to control nicotine levels.

Officially scribed minutes from this conference totalled eighteen pages. When these reached corporate executives at Brown & Williamson, Dr. Wigand describes their reaction as "apoplectic". Eighteen pages of professional meetings attended by some of the best educated scientific minds in the world were edited by B & W lawyers, and condensed to three pages. All reference to the addictiveness of nicotine and suggestions to develop a safe cigarette disappeared from the pages of these minutes. Tobacco lawyers decided any reference to development of a safe cigarette implied the existing product is dangerous, and such material could be used in discovery for liability action against them. From that point, lawyers attended all scientific research meetings and decided who would have access to research documents.

Dr. Wigand advocated the removal of coumarin from pipe tobacco. Coumarin is a rat poison and had been removed from cigarettes after research confirmed liver toxicity it caused to dogs, and the U.S. National Toxicology Program released evidence it is a lung specific car

cinogen. It continues today to be added to pipe tobacco as a scent
enhancer. He was told if science adversely affected sales, science would
take the back door. It could be said with certainty that the internal
policy for Brown & Williamson was Sales Over Safety. Every time.

On March 24, 1993, Thomas Sandefur, CEO of Brown &
Williamson Tobacco, terminated the employment of Dr. Jeffrey Wigand,
Corporate Vice President and Director of Research and Development.
To support his family, Dr. Wigand became a high school teacher (and
obtained a M.Sc. Degree in Teaching from the University of Louis-
ville). His new career as a teacher coincided with the beginning of
over three years of intimidation and death threats directed towards Dr.
Wigand – simply, for telling the truth.

In 1994, Mississippi filed a lawsuit against the tobacco industry to
recover the substantial costs required to treat patients for disease caused
by tobacco, and Dr. Wigand provided significant information about
tobacco's mandate of profits-at-any-cost. At Dr. Wigand's initial deposition, he was able to provide only minutes of testimony amid four
hours of objections from some of the two hundred tobacco lawyers
attending. Kentucky courtrooms have their own rules about defectors
from tobacco, and defendant Wigand was permitted only two attorneys while the tobacco cartel had fifty, and were linked electronically
to thirty more. The documentary about this trial, produced by *60 Minutes*, would not air as scheduled. This well-respected news source buck-
led under pressure from the tobacco cartel's intimidation to Shut Up.
Tobacco Justice apparently also has on its payroll judges in Kentucky
who are allowed to make personal threats to defense attorneys protecting the civil rights of their client whose testimony is not in the best
interest of Big Tobacco.

Big Tobacco does not take kindly to exposure of dirty secrets. The
Wall Street Journal dismantled the worst attempt at a smear campaign
they said they'd ever seen. Their independent investigators took the 500
pages of misinformation about Dr. Wigand, provided to them by tobacco lawyers, checked out every allegation and found them all to be
false. The story hit the Wall Street Journal front page. Despite the tobacco cartel's best efforts they failed to blacken Dr. Wigand's reputation. Tobacco made no mention of what they thought about Dr. Wigand
being honored with only 51 other teachers across the U.S. in 1996 when
he received the Sallie Mae First Class Teacher of the Year Award.

Michael Mann, Director of the movie "The Insider" received threats on a regular basis from the tobacco industry to stop production of the movie. Dr. Wigand's vehicle was 'accidentally' broadsided by an eighteen-wheeler on the freeway. A bullet appeared in his mailbox and threats were issued against his daughters.

Because of Dr. Wigand, lay people learned a little basic tobacco chemistry – for example, how ammonia – a common cleaning chemical emitting toxic fumes - is deliberately added to tobacco, to change nicotine from a salt into a free base. Dr. Wigand's honesty means that smokers now understand how acetalehyde acts as an impact booster, augmenting the effect of nicotine. He leaves no doubt that cigarettes are anything but a natural product – they are meticulously engineered Nicotine Delivery Devices, marketed with the help of cowboys and cartoons . An internal slogan at B & W has become public, a daily affirmation they are in the nicotine delivery business, and tar is the negative baggage. Dr. Wigand explains in easy-to-understand language how nicotine is a binding substance that affects brain receptors. Each fix of nicotine releases the fight-or-flight neurotransmitter called dopamine that begs for a repeat performance and builds dependency (a.k.a. addiction).

We also learned why none of the tobacco executives smoke. When a Winston cigarette model noticed none of the R.J. Reynolds executives smoked during a meeting, he asked why. The answer?

"We don't smoke the shit. We just sell it. We reserve the right to smoke for the young, the poor, the black and the stupid." (3)

Tobacco's decision to fund philanthropic community projects such as shelters for battered women followed extensive research into how easily these targets would become addicted to their product. For every $1 Philip Morris spend to "make a difference" – in projects such as food and supplies for war-torn eastern European countries, where they also distribute free cigarettes to 14-year olds (4) - they spend $1.30 to advertise their brand of philanthropy in prime-time TV slots. If "making a difference" were truly their mandate, they could immediately cease manufacturing a product that when used for its sole intended purpose, results in addiction, disease, suffering and death.

Dr. Wigand teaches more, however, than high school chemistry. His example of ethics over money shows up Big Tobacco in a very unflattering light. Dr. Wigand forfeited a dream job as his discomfort over his employer's product boomeranged when his young daughters asked him why he worked for someone who killed people. His real-life struggle, and what it means to lose 30 years of life's work and hard earned financial security, speaks clearly that the deceit has to stop.

Dr. Wigand has provided a living illustration of how telling the truth survives intimidation, deceit and fraud.

"Foul, rotten rubber...Strong Tongue Sting and Throat Grab...Nicotine is definitely an irritant in smoke and its taste must be blended out or modified by other constituents in the TPM [total particulate matter] to make the smoke acceptable."
From *Taste of Nicotine* (C.E. RIx), a section of the 10-Page "Nicotine Research" memo (Nov. 9, 1976), written by W.M. Henley, and addressed to Dr. D.H. Piehl, which summarized an Oct. 25, 1976 discussion of nicotine Trial Exhibit #TE10539, 12673

James Repace, Health Physicist

"The National Toxicology Program now includes mustard gas, asbestos and arsenic in the same category as tobacco smoke. You don't want to go near any of those." (James Repace)

James Repace obtained a B.Sc. Physics from Polytechnic Institute of Brooklyn in 1962 and an M.Sc. in Physics in 1968. He completed post-masters study in Physics at the University of Maryland in 1969 and at Catholic University 1970-1972. From 1987 – 1989 he was a member of the Surgeon General's National Advisory Panel on Smoking & Health and from 1987 to present has been a member of the World Health Organization Expert Advisory Panel on Tobacco or Health. From 1994 – 2000 he was a member of the Scientific Peer-Review Panel, University of California Tobacco-Related Disease Program.

James Repace's contribution to raising public awareness about tobacco and secondhand smoke began in 1980 when he identified secondhand smoke as a major source of indoor air pollution, and the greatest source of population exposure to respirable particulate air pollution. His paper attracted international interest from the global scientific community. (5) James Repace uses the foundation of his own formal education and a career in research physics to speak out about the very real risk to human health posed by tobacco smoke. The National Toxicology Program have now included tobacco smoke, tobacco smoking and smokeless tobacco in their Ninth Report on Carcinogens, revised in January 2001. This report lists contains "Profiles for Agents, Substances, Mixtures or Exposure Circumstances Known To Be Human Carcinogens" . (6) Tobacco smoke, tobacco smoking and smokeless tobacco now claim the distinction of being classified in the same category as mustard gas, asbestos, arsenic and benzene as known cancer-causing agents.

"The Evidence to Date...Obviously the amount of evidence accumulated to indict cigarette smoke as a health hazard is overwhelming. The evidence challenging such an indictment is scant." **1962 R. J. Reynolds report by Alan Rodgman,** *The Smoking and Health Problem - a critical and objective appraisal of.* **Trial Exhibit 18187. This document was discussed in the Minnesota trial on January 29, 1998, March 6, 1998, March 30, 1998 and March 31, 1998.**

Patrick Reynolds, grandson of tobacco founder R.J. Reynolds speaks out against tobacco

"When my grandfather began manufacturing cigarettes at the turn of the [20th] century, he did not know that smoking causes lung disease, heart disease and cancer. Now that this has been absolutely proven, I want to help people wake up to how addictive and poisonous cigarettes are." (Patrick J. Reynolds)

Patrick Reynolds, heir to the R.J. Reynolds tobacco fortune, watched tobacco kill his grandfather, mother, father , two aunts and his brother. The two family brands, *Camel* and *Winston* that made the Reynolds clan wealthy also killed off beloved family members, picking them off one at a time with various cancers and emphysema. He divested his inheritance of R. J. Reynolds stock and in 1989 founded the Los Angeles based Citizens for a Smoke-Free America. He speaks loudly about how the tobacco cartel abuses the Bill of Rights in their quest to advertise their product, especially to children. He reminds his audiences that Philip Morris spent tens of millions of dollars touring the Bill of Rights around the United States, encouraging school children to view it – complete, of course, with the Philip Morris logo. Their attempts never falter to shift the focus away from the devastating health consequences from use of their product to personal freedom issues (except if you are a nonsmoker because then your freedom not to smoke, according to tobacco, takes a poor second place to the rights of smokers to consume Philip Morris products at any time or place they choose).

Patrick Reynolds was born into wealth and privilege. When he became aware of the terrible price paid by those whose addiction created his family's fortune, he disassociated himself from any further contact with the industry.

"One of the striking features of the Auerbach experiment was that practically every dog which smoked suffered significantly from the effects of the smoke either in terms of severe irritation and bronchitis, pre-cancerous changes, or cancer." "[We] believe that the Auerbach work proves beyond reasonable doubt that fresh whole cigarette smoke is carcinogenic to dog lungs and therefore it is highly likely that it is carcinogenic to human lungs." "[T]he results of the research would appear to us to remove the controversy regarding the causation of human lung cancer although it does not help us directly with the problem of how to modify our cigarettes." April 3, 1970 Gallagher memo, American Tobacco's British-based sister company. Trial Exhibit 21,905

Joe Cherner

"Comic books – good and evil. Very simple. The tobacco cartel are evil. " (Joe Cherner)

In 1986, Joe Cherner left a million-dollar-a-year job on Wall Street to retire on investment income, lobby actively for increased tobacco control and found Smoke Free Educational Services in New York. He testified as an expert witness in the Engle trial in Florida in the summer of the year 2000 where $145 billion punitive damages were awarded to plaintiffs in a class action suit by Florida residents suffering from tobacco-related diseases (Howard Engle who suffered from emphysema was originally the lead plaintiff). In New York City and New York State he has been instrumental in the passing of meaningful smoke-free legislation. In 1987 a law was passed segregating smoking sections as distinct from smoke-free sections in restaurants. He worked to enact the law prohibiting distribution of free cigarettes – cigarettes can no longer be given out free to anyone, for any reason in New York

City. He worked to eliminate the sale of cigarettes in vending machines. He worked to eliminate the sale of individual cigarettes, or "loosies". Schools in New York City are now tobacco free – no tobacco use by anyone on any school property. He worked to increase excise tax on cigarettes in 1995 to 56 cents, at the time the highest in the U.S. Also in 1995 he worked to pass the law to make dining areas of virtually all New York City restaurants smoke-free. The seating areas of all outdoor sports stadiums in New York are now smoke-free. Outdoor playgrounds in New York City are now smoke free. Tobacco pollution in New York City taxis has been eliminated A law has been passed requiring counter advertising space on all city property where tobacco was advertised and tobacco advertising has now become illegal on all subway cars, platforms, entrances, buses, shelters, telephone booths, ferries, airports and all city owned billboards in the city of New York. A lawsuit was filed to stop the Marlboro Grand Prix from happening in New York City and an additional lawsuit was filed to take down the Marlboro billboard in Shea Stadium. Legislation was passed in 1999 eliminating any tobacco advertising visible from the street (including push-pull stickers on glass doors) and is currently under appeal. Cigarette excise tax in New York currently totals $1.11, again the highest in the U.S.

He has organized a protest at Philip Morris' headquarters led by a rabbi, a priest and a minister whose followers, 200 school children, carried signs saying "Thou Shalt Not Kill".

He pointed out very succinctly to some visiting executives from Philip Morris the idiocy of their claims about smoke-free legislation harming business when he said, *"When the buses went from having separate smoking sections to being smoke-free, there was talk that smokers wouldn't take public transportation. When the movie theatres here in New York City went from having separate smoking sections to being smoke-free, the tobacco cartel said smokers would not go to the movies because they couldn't sit for two hours without a cigarette and the movie theatres would go out of business. When the baseball stadiums around the country went smoke-free and every single one was smoke-free for the 1995 season, the tobacco cartel said smokers would not renew their season's tickets. When the airlines went smoke-free, and the trains went smoke-free, from having separate smoking sections – the tobacco cartel said smokers wouldn't take trains or planes anymore, they would drive. Well, all the heads of the tobacco cartel*

came to New York City for our hearings from Albany, from Washing-
ton, from Virginia – and they all came on smoke-free transportation."

After fifteen years, during which Joe Cherner claims he has earned
no income but achieved substantial outcome, he has worked successfully to gain significant progress in the enactment of smoke-free legislation and has participated in an historical lawsuit resulting in the biggest punitive damages ever awarded against tobacco. Mr. Cherner gives
the strong impression he has only just completed a warm-up.

**"I have become more and more convinced that we should not con-
duct any longevity studies with animals. It appears to me that even
positive results would be meaningless in light of the human experience where statistical evidence indicates that longevity is adversely
affected by smoking." December 21, 1976 PM document,** *Longevity Study with Animals,* **from Dr. Seligman to Jett Lincoln   Trial
Exhibit 11470**

THE "AIN'TS"

Ain't: a contraction for *are not, is not, has not,* **and** *have not* **; a
stigmatization** (American Heritage Dictionary of the English Language)

When considering any virtue, the word "ain't" whose meaning con-
denses to "not" accurately reflects those who promote and profit from
a product which, when used for its sole intended purpose, results in
addiction, disease, suffering and miserable death. The Ain'ts definitely
conform to stigmatized versions of the Saints.

Dr. Gio Batta Gori

**"Birth-rate declines may correlate with increased sales of nylon
hosiery, but is the association causal?"** *(Science, Imaginable Risks,
and Public Policy: Anatomy of a Mirage, Gio Batta Gori February
15, 1996)*

Dr. Gio Gori, former Deputy Director of the U.S. National Cancer Institute, has worked as an "independent tobacco consultant" since
1980. His tobacco affiliation became publicly acknowledged during
the Minnesota trial when previously secret tobacco documents surfaced.
In one, he aggressively enquired whether or not tobacco could use their

influence to obtain a political appointment for him. As part of Project Whitecoat, he accepted payment from the tobacco industry to sign letters prepared by their lawyers and sent to respected medical journals to maintain controversy over damaging confirmation from the Environmental Protection Agency that secondhand smoke is carcinogenic. He received US$4,000 for one such letter published in *The Lancet.* (7)

When Richard Horton, Editor of *The Lancet,* learned of Dr. Gori's tobacco-financed opinion, he said "Gori has breached a bond of trust as a scientist between himself and the scientific community. This is at best unethical and at worst an example of research misconduct." (8)

The tobacco-friendly Fraser Institute published a book co-authored by Gio Gori attempting to dismantle the scientific efforts of the U.S. Environmental Protection Agency and their conclusion about second-hand smoke qualifying as a Class A carcinogen. When asked about his tobacco-funded opinions, Gio Gori responded defensively and angrily by saying, "Are you getting paid for what you're writing? We're all out there working".(9) This former Deputy Director of the U.S. National Cancer Institute has some final words on the subject of the avoidable health risks of exposure to secondhand smoke: "The smoker's right to smoke is being impeded upon in a smoke-free society. Environmental tobacco smoke is an unavoidable nuisance, but there is no link between (secondhand smoke) and an increased risk of lung cancer." (10)

The Research Directors of Philip Morris, Liggett & Myers and R.J. Reynolds also participated. Their priority focused on keeping current with information about government interference in the tobacco industry, and had no perceivable interest in the development of a less dangerous cigarette. Standing alone against the opinions of peer scientists who have not sold out to the tobacco cartel, Gori stubbornly maintained the development of a safe cigarette remained possible.

It takes only one tobacco scientist to instigate "debate" among members of the lay public, especially smokers who do not want to hear secondhand smoke harms their children and spouses. Gio Gori has become a pariah among his professional peers.

"Boy! Wouldn't it be wonderful if our company was first to produce a cancer-free cigarette. What we could do to the competition!" Mid-1950s Hill & Knowlton memo quoting an unnamed tobacco company research director   Trial Exhibit TE18904

Theodor and Elia Sterling

"As recently as 1997, Philip Morris paid Elia Sterling $87,000 for work to be performed by Theodor Sterling...the tobacco industry is intimately involved with current so-called 'ventilation solutions' being authored by Elia Sterling". *(Controlling Globally, Acting Locally, Physicians for a Smoke-Free Canada, June 2000)*

Theodor Sterling engineered reports in the 1960's and 1970's implying division existed within the scientific community regarding the health consequences of smoking, and repeated the exercise in the 1980's and 1990's concerning exposure to secondhand smoke. A research professor at Simon Fraser University in Vancouver, Canada, Theodor Sterling set up his own private consulting firm, well established on the tobacco payroll. Between 1973 and 1990, over $5 million from the Council for Tobacco Research (a front group for tobacco multinationals) funded Theodor Sterling's promotion of tobacco interests. (11) His mandate appeared to remain unflinching: exploit any cause of lung cancer as long as it is nothing to do with secondhand smoke. Occupational hazards? Many. Genetic predisposition? Of course. Tobacco smoke? "Unproven". Maintain the tobacco cartel propaganda that the perils of life on Planet Earth include anything you can think of – except, of course, tobacco use and exposure to tobacco smoke. (12)

"Wherever possible we should seek to arrange for all smoking and health matters to be dealth with through an association of all members of the [tobacco] industry." BAT internal memo 1972 *Smoking and Health.* **Bates No. 302058848**

Kenneth Clarke

"One of the most advanced and responsible British companies I have come across." *(Kenneth Clarke's description of British American Tobacco Company, BBC U.K. Politics, June 27, 2001)*

Earning £100,000 annually in the position of Deputy Chairman of British American Tobacco Company, Kenneth Clark vigorously promoted a £28 million cigarette production deal in Vietnam. Despite the World Health Organization advocacy for global tobacco control, Kenneth Clark toils earnestly for his personal tobacco paymaster before the competition has had the opportunity to make inroads in a poor country, whose government concerns itself more with tobacco revenue than the safety of consumer products and the health and welfare of its citizens. He claims that British American Tobacco are "squeaky clean" and are a paragon of good corporate citizenship with "high ethical standards". British American Tobacco's "high ethical standards" and "squeaky clean" business involve admission of exploitation of tobacco smuggling operations and an investigation into participation in organized crime in the U.S. (13)

Currently a back-bench Conservative Member of Parliament, and former Chancellor in the Thatcher government, Kenneth Clarke entertains notions of leadership of the Conservative party to the chagrin and embarrassment of his colleagues, one of whom was quoted as saying "Only Ken could run for the Tory leadership while sitting in Hanoi peddling cigarettes to the Vietnamese. Any of the rest of us selling ciggies to the third world would be torn apart by the press". (14)

"At the best, the probabilities are that some combination of constituents of smoke will be found conducive to the onset of cancer or to create an environment in which cancer is more likely to occur." Addison Yeaman, vice president and general counsel Brown & Williamson, 1963 Document i.d. 1802.05, page 1 *The Cigarette Papers*

Scott Goddard (University of Nottingham, U.K.)

"Grow up." (Senior Lecturer, Director of Postgraduate Programmes and Director of Modular MBA, Scott Goddard's reply to a letter of protest about Nottingham University's acceptance in December 2000 of £3.8 million from British American Tobacco to build a School of Business Ethics)

Despite public outrage and a British Medical Journal opinion poll 84% in support of rejection of tobacco funding, Nottingham University accepted £3.8 million from British American Tobacco. (15) The funding provided by BATCO to Nottingham University has been earmarked for the implementation of a School of Business Ethics, at a time when BATCO is the current object of a Trade and Industry inquiry and is being sued in the U.S. for participating in organized crime, and is answering to racketeering charges in Ecuador and Colombia. (16)

Does Nottingham University require the American equivalent of nearly $7 million to teach business ethics sponsored by the antithesis of any standard of decency?

Six months following the acceptance of tobacco blood money, sixteen research staff resigned from Nottingham University to move to London University. (17) The Cancer Research Campaign spends more on research in universities and colleges than any other charity, including £1.5m at Nottingham. Following Nottingham University's decision, they withdrew their support and their £1.4 million annual grant has come under scrutiny. (18)

The editor of the *British Medical Journal* resigned from his position at Nottingham University as honorary professor, and Mel Read, a graduate of Nottingham University and member of the European parliament, resigned her position as special lecturer at Nottingham. Jon Rouse, a Nottingham University MBA graduate refused to accept his cash prize for Student of the Year award, requesting it be donated to cancer research.

Kenneth Clarke, Member of Parliament for Nottinghamshire and on BATCO's payroll for £100,000 a year as their Deputy Chairman, supported Nottingham University's acceptance of tobacco money.

Nottingham University has earned the rightful reputation of Tobacco U. The disgrace of being in tobacco's pocket was donated free of charge.

"A respected polling institution will be hired in 1991 to run "counter-surveys" when necessary...For example, if the WHO claims that 75% of the people want smoking bans on international flights, we can counter with our own survey. Since the polling firm will be responsible for dissemination, the poll will gain credibility." "Commission a video of the future when drinking milk is only by prescription." Philip Morris Tobacco Company's strategic plans to fight workplace smoking bans in Europe, December 1990 Bates No. 2026097515/7541

The Original Junkscientist

"No one really knows what causes asthma. It must be difficult to rule out confounding risk factors when you don't know what they are." *(Steven Milloy, Secondhand Smoke and Asthma in Kids 1998)*

A self-described "adjunct scholar" of the tobacco-friendly, libertarian "think tank" going by the name of the Cato Institute, Steven Milloy chose the term well to describe his web page: Junk Science. Junk science accurately describes uninformed opinion of any detailed medical and scientific data contrary to the bought and paid-for tobacco agenda.

A former Executive Director of a tobacco-fronted organization calling itself The Advancement of Sound Science Coalition (TASSC), Mr. Milloy's background exists in the number crunching career of the biostatistics of science and a law degree. His education includes a B.A. in Natural Sciences from Johns Hopkins University, a Master of Health Sciences in Biostatistics from the Johns Hopkins University School of Hygiene and Public Health, a Juris Doctorate from the University of Baltimore, and a Master of Laws from the Georgetown University Law Center.

His career centers around tobacco lobbying, number-juggling and cursory dissections of world-class scientific and medical research by globally accepted experts. Tobacco buries itself deeply to escape discovery of connection to its front groups. Milloy worked as director of science policy studies at the National Environmental Policy Institute - a part of The Center for Strategic and International Studies, funded by the Center for Strategic and International Studies (CSIS), who in turn receives direction and funding from Philip Morris board member, Harold Brown who lists this organization on his resume.

Serious scientists can expect a hearty chuckle or two upon visiting the junkscience web page talking about "fear profiteers" and a desire to "inform the public". Don't expect to find the truth about nicotine addiction and the ravages caused by tobacco consumption. The where-will-it-all-end fear-mongering about non-existent threats against civil liberties and alleged victimization/hatred/exploitation of smokers does nothing to camouflage tobacco's efforts to promote their flailing image of smoking as a social norm.

"To summarize, the direction we are headed will be to deflect this [ETS] issue, to redefine it, to broaden it, to demonstrate as we have in the case of accidental fires and youth behavior that we are contributing to the solution rather than to the problem...." Report on Public Smoking Issue Executive Committee April 10, (confidential) by William Kloepfer of the Tobacco Institute Recipient: Tobacco Institute Executive Committee Bates No. TIMN0013710-372

John "Fraser Institute" Luik

"What is so morally offensive here is that truly morally blameless people - not the alleged victims of smokers - but smokers themselves, are to be harmed in significant ways on the basis of bogus science and for no good reason." *(John Luik)*

John Luik was born in Portland Oregon in 1950 and attended Oxford University on a Rhodes Scholarship. Before he completed his studies for a Ph.D. in Philosophy and had earned the right to do so, he called himself "Dr. Luik". When the lies on his resume were discovered he was dismissed from his post at Nazarene College in Winnipeg where he had worked from 1977 to 1985. He completed his doctoral studies in 1986 in disciplines unrelated to medical science. In 1985 he applied at Brock University where he taught applied and professional ethics. Did his curriculum include techniques in how not to get caught when lying about professional qualifications?

Brock University knew of his earlier deception but once his doctorate was completed in 1986, administration there decided to overlook one mistake and give him another chance. What had been hoped to have been a single incident of poor judgement, however, became John Luik's norm. "It is not any single misrepresentation ... so much as the apparently uniform pattern of misrepresentations engaged in since 1977 that suggests that Professor Luik is not capable of fulfilling his duties and responsibilities as an assistant professor at Brock University," a 17-page faculty report says. Further information contained in the same report reveals that John Luik showed "no particular signs of contrition or even embarrassment on being confronted with his misrepresentation. This suggested that what was involved was indeed faulty moral judgment". (19)

John Luik falsely claimed he had held a full-time position at the University of Manitoba, and taught three graduate courses at the University of Winnipeg. Not only had he never worked at the University of Manitoba, but one of the graduate courses he claimed to have taught at the University of Winnipeg was non-existent. According to the university's official statement, no graduate courses in philosophy have ever been offered. Cecil Abrahams, former Dean of Humanities at Brock University and currently the Chancellor of South Africa's University of West Cape said John Luik's shameful misrepresentations are "worst case of fraud that I had come across and I've been an administrator at universities for a long period of time". (20)

Is it surprising that someone who has earned the reputation of an impressive fraud would be approached by the tobacco cartel to dispute any information contrary to tobacco's interests?

Those who profit from the sale of addictive drugs typically do not use their products. John Luik does not smoke. He claims smokers choose to smoke and nicotine is not addictive. At a Fraser Institute lecture in April, 1999 John Luik admitted he is on the tobacco payroll and this self-proclaimed teacher of business ethics stated he sees nothing amiss with accepting money from an industry to conduct dispassionate "research" while promoting tobacco products which, when used as directed, sicken and kill those who pay to consume it.

Dr. Luik is a doctor of philosophy, not medicine. He steadfastly claims secondhand smoke poses minimal health risks. He likes to talk about "risk analysis" and professes to care about personal choices (although those who choose to be smoke-free seem to be curiously ignored). He fuels the tobacco fronted fire alleging some kind of nefarious conspiracy by the medical profession to prevent a legal business from peddling its product for use without restriction by consenting adults. He likes to use the metaphor of David and Goliath – with the tobacco cartel as a cowed and victimized David. His line of thinking has been referred to as neanderthal by his scientific betters, who he accuses of having no common sense. When doctors of philosophy can diagnose 90% of lung cancer cases in smokers and ex-smokers the way doctors of medicine at the Harvard School of Medicine do, perhaps the philosophers will be taken seriously when opining from their tobacco funded think tanks about the "harmless habit" of smoking. John Luik's career is punctuated with lies, fraud and harsh censure from those whose trust he violated. The tobacco cartel chose well when selecting John Luik to pay him to represent their interests.

His comments as they appear for a tobacco front group, on honesty - from someone with tarnished integrity: "The frightening thing about deceit - whether in the allegedly righteous cause of eliminating smoking or in the service of any number of other worthy ends - is both that it is so easy to justify and so difficult to restrict its use to the ends that originally justified its employment."

"The exposure Marlboro received from this movie is worth something, but not $200M. If I had to assign a value it would be $100M.

The placement is not worth $200M because the actual logo is not seen"
Brown & Williamson Tobacco agreed the placement of Marlboro
Cigarettes in the movie *Apocalypse Now* was worth $100M for the
advertising it provided.   document number 2403.01, Brown &
Williamson Document, by N. Domanty, 1983

Sylvester Stallone

"Rambo isn't violent. I see Rambo as a philantropist." *(Sylvester
Stallone, Today, London May 1988)*

   Young people especially look to movie stars for role models. Unfortunately some movie stars care more for the hefty payments they receive
for advertising tobacco products disguised as acting props than they do
about the message they impart to their young, impressionable fans.

"April 28, 1983
Mr. Bob Kovoloff
Associated Film Promotion
10100 Santa Monica Blvd.,
Los Angeles, California 90067

Dear Bob,

As discussed, I guarantee that I will use Brown & Williamson
tobacco products in no less than five feature films.
It is my understanding that Brown & Williamson will pay a fee of
$500,000.00.
Hoping to hear from you soon.
Sincerely,
Sylvester Stallone" (21)

   When tobacco is promoted to millions in a captive audience via the
movie industry it is called product placement: intentional placement
of tobacco products in exchange for cash payment or other material
incentives.
   In The Muppet Movie, (G rated entertainment primarily for children ten years of age and under), three of the human characters have
cigarettes in their mouths: a bartender, a used car salesman and a Hollywood tycoon. Other movies in which Philip Morris admitted they

supplied tobacco products include *Airplane, American Hot , California Suite, Cannery Row, Chu Chu & The Philly Flash, Cloak & Dagger, Coat To Coast, Coma, Continental Divide, Crocodile Dundee, Deal Of The Century, Disorderlies, Doing Time On Planet Earth, Dream Team, Foul Play, Grease, Hero At Large, Hurricane, I Ought to be in Pictures, Invaders From Mars, Jaws II, Jimmy the Kid, Little Shop of Horrors, Love At First Site, Miracles, Mommy Dearest, Mr. Mom, My Favorite Year, Nightwing, Opening Night, Paradise Alley, Pray TV, Rocky II, Romantic Comedy, Second Chance, Sleepaway Lump, Steel, Student Memories, The Avengers, The Baltimore Outlet, The Champ, The Fish That Saved Pittsburgh, The In-Laws, The Wrong Guys, Trust Me, Who Framed, Roger Rabbit, Without a Trace.*

Included in Philip Morris' admitted "product placement is *"Danny Lavine Always Has A Good Time"* — rated best children's script by the Writers' Guild , produced for and shown by PBS. (22)

Summary

Many more saints exist than there is room to talk about them. The famous names of Dr. Stanton Glantz, Dr. Stella Bialous, Drs. Kessler, Koop, Anne Landman, Gene Borio, Stan Shatenstein , join Canadians who work to treat nicotine addiction: Dr. Fred Bass, Dr. Ray Baker, Dr. Lorna Medd and their colleagues. Neil Collishaw and Cynthia Callard who work tirelessly with the Physicians for a Smoke-Free Canada provide cheerful and reliable resource material about all aspects of tobacco, from the profit per cigarette to the poisons a waitress in a smoky bar must breathe during her shift. Many countless saints work quietly and effectively and those highlighted here represent thousands more who share the goal to tell the truth about tobacco.

Anyone who places tobacco profits over people qualifies unconditionally as an "ain't".

"I'll tell you why I like the cigarette business. It costs a penny to make. Sell it for a dollar. It's addictive. And there's fantastic brand loyalty." (R.J. Reynolds stockholder)

• III - TOBACCO BRAND OF SCIENCE •
Hire Scientists Who Will Make It So

"The question is," said Alice, "whether you can make words mean so many different things." "The question is," said Humpty Dumpty, "which is to be master – that's all." Lewis Carroll, *Through the Looking-Glass*. "We are in a nicotine rather than a tobacco industry." *Project Mad Hatter*, B&W 1971

Think of the proverbial bottomless pit and you have an accurate picture of tobacco resources. In the U.S. the tobacco industry spend $22.5 million every day on advertising and they also maintain endless reserves for teams of lawyers and scientists who are paid to protect tobacco interests by whatever means necessary.

The tobacco industry do not need to win any debate about the health consequences of using their product. Continuation of controversy maintains a level of doubt which, in their well voiced and heavily financed public statements, has not and will never be fully resolved. They remain unique in this viewpoint. Their own damning documents have now connected with the light of day and their shameful organized campaigns of deception and manipulation have become a matter of public record.

Shockerwick Shame

The conspiracy between R.J. Reynolds, British-American Tobacco, Rothmans, Reetsma, Philip Morris and the U.K. tobacco companies Gallagher and Imperial, dates back to 1977. The documents leave no doubt about their strategy, executed with military precision and millions of dollars, to maintain controversy about the health consequences of smoking and conceal what all tobacco research scientists knew: nicotine is addictive.

The conspiracy consisted mainly of an agreement between individual tobacco industry members, uniting to dismantle any connection between smoking and disease. Each agreed not to promote their product as 'safer' than their competitors, because combined denial of negative health consequences of tobacco use meant credibility for the industry. Also, any mention of a "safer cigarette" carries the clear implication that cigarettes in the past posed dangers and opened a dangerous door to future litigation.

On December 3, 1976, Tony Garrett, Chairman of Imperial Tobacco in London, England (referred to as "TG" in the memorandum) telephoned Hugh Cullman, President of Philip Morris at the time. This phone call generated a confidential internal Philip Morris memorandum entitled "Operation Berkshire" suggesting a meeting at Shockerwick Hall in England. (2)

"The meeting would be as discreet as possible with, hopefully, no publicity emanating therefrom, with a public affairs statement ready should news of such a meeting leak out."

"The initial objective of this group was to include a smoking and health strategy which would include a voluntary agreement that no concessions beyond a certain point would be made by the members and if further concessions were required by respective governments, that these not be agreed to and that governments be forced to legislate. TG seemed to be most concerned that companies and countries would be picked off one by one and that the Domino theory would impact on all of us"

On March 24, 1977 Tony Garrett wrote to Philip Morris outlining the names of the attendees , offers of arrangements for golf and other tourist activities and enclosing a press release deliberately misrepresenting the purpose of the gathering (3)

"We have also prepared for your comment a draft statement which could be used in the unlikely event of our meeting becoming known to the Press. There is general agreement we should make every effort to maintain tight security over our meeting, but we need to be prepared for the possibility of a leak."

"You may consider it prudent to distribute this paper to the various participants in advance and if you do may I ask you to stress the need for confidentiality and security as neither Philip Morris nor ourselves would wish this paper to fall into the wrong hands."

The "Position Paper" outlined the terms of the proposed voluntary agreement among participating tobacco companies. (4)

"We acknowledge the fact that there is a continuing smoking and health controversy but we do not accept as proven there is a causal relationship between smoking and various diseases (such as lung cancer, heart disease, bronchitis etc.). In our view the issue of causation remains controversial and unresolved."

"To be effective it is desirable that the tobacco industry as a whole must be seen to be responsible and, within our field, authoritative.

Moreover we believe it is better to speak as an industry with one voice on such matters and this can best be accomplished through national associations of manufacturers."

The "Position Paper" states clear intentions of influencing medical information (Operation Whitecoat will be discussed later). (5)

"We should influence as far as possible medical and official opinion against incautious imposition of constraints and any unnecessary restrictions on smoking."

As if peering 23 years into a crystal ball, manufacturers of tobacco products in 1977 state the intention of fierce resistance to package warnings about tobacco use (6)

"If Governments suggest wording implying or stating that smoking causes certain diseases, Companies must strenuously resist with all means at their disposal."

Accountability for manipulation of addictive nicotine and harmful tar in their product was as unwelcome in 1977 as it is today. (7)

"The imposition of maximum tar and nicotine yields, as well as attempts to tax high tar products differentially to those with lower deliveries, should be resisted.

"We should resist any requirements to put figures for the yields of smoke constituents or tar groups on packs or in advertising."

The initial Shockerwick conference resulted in working parties who called themselves The International Committee on Smoking Issues. Without exception, all members represented the tobacco industry. Honor among liars can exist. Initial fallout prevented progress when the three British delegates would not concede that no causal relationship between smoking and disease exists. A memo from Dr. Helmut Geisch (Philip Morris Research and Development) to two top Philip Morris scientists bemoaned the lack of agreement between members.(8)

"...it was very difficult to embark on a constructive discussion at all as the philosophies differed so widely. In addition, I got the impression that some people really lived in 'cloud cuckoo land' because many of the proposed research ideas went out of the way to produce experimental results which would be biased against the cigarette. Especially Dr. Field tended to bend over backward in proposing smoking conditions to be imposed on experimental animals which were so severe that they could not be taken as representative of the human situation. He belongs to the school of scientists who want to get 'clear cut end-points', no matter what they mean."

Just over a year later, on June 28, 1977, the first violation of the voluntary agreement between international tobacco companies divided the members. British American Tobacco Chairman Stewart Lockhart wrote a recriminatory letter to Philip Morris for agreeing to publication of tar and nicotine content in Norway and therefore, by disclosing the truth about cigarettes, breaking the agreement. (9)

"I have learned with some considerable concern that your company has issued a tar/nicotine league table to the tobacco retail trade in Norway."

"I am most concerned that your Company should have seen fit to breach this understanding and more particularly so as it would seem to go against if not the letter then certainly the spirit of our joint Companies' position as accepted by the I.C.O.S.I. group."

"Moreover, by this action you are setting a most unwelcome precedent, which does not augur well for future co-operation between our two companies on Smoking and Health matters."

Compare the stubborn allegation that smoking does not necessarily make smokers sick, with the sentiment expressed in a February 1978 memorandum from T.S. Osdene, Director of Research for Philip Morris in the U.S.:

". . . an admission by the industry that excessive cigarette smoking is bad for you is tantamount to an admission of guilt with regard to the lung cancer problem. This could open the door to legal suits in which the industry would have no defence." (10)

157 such tobacco documents surfaced in the search conducted by Neil Francey and Simon Chapman when they documented their findings about an organized tobacco conspiracy in the British Medical Journal (11)

On May 8, 1998 The Minnesota District Court ordered American tobacco companies to place online previously confidential company letters and memoranda. This information now adds up to over thirty million pages of internal documents.

"Smoking bans are the biggest challenge we have ever faced. Quit rate goes from 5% to 21% when smokers work in nonsmoking environments." (Handwritten Philip Morris 1994 memo *ETS World Conference* Bates Number 2054893642)

The Chelsea Group

Philip Morris' own painstaking research illustrates the reason for their resistance to smoking regulations: quit rates quadruple when workers are prohibited from smoking in their workplaces.

The tobacco industry claim adequate ventilation accommodates smokers and nonsmokers who can happily co-exist in the same room. They use terms like "dilution ventilation" and "displacement ventilation" in their attempts to convince public health authorities about the "non-issue" of secondhand smoke. Nobody else agrees with this point of view except a tiny minority of smokers. Research physicist James Repace, who worked as policy analyst and staff scientist for the Environmental Protection Agency confirms the velocity of a tornado is required to create smoke-free conditions from a smoky room.

The Chelsea Group states on its official Internet homepage *"Chelsea Group, Ltd. is an Illinois Corporation, created by George Benda, who serves as its Chairman and Chief Executive Officer."* (12) George Benda is listed in *The Chelsea Group "Our People"* as "Senior Principal, Chairman and CEO... an industry leading consultant well known for his strategic insights, indoor air quality (IAQ) product development, training skills and IAQ assessment leadership. He is regularly sought by industry leaders to help clients create strategic initiatives, develop new products and introduce services to grow their IAQ related businesses".

"Broadly respected for his IAQ problem solving, Mr. Benda has led teams in a wide range of indoor environment investigations and has used that expertise in working to shape effective standards applicable in creating healthy indoor environments. His training skills have been recognized by the Association of Energy Engineers, who awarded Mr. Benda the Environmental Educator of the Year for 1996, and by IAQ Publications, who awarded him Indoor Environment Trainer of the Year for 1997. A dynamic speaker, George is a frequent presenter at international conferences on a wide range of IAQ issues".

Other principals in The Chelsea Group list their professional degrees in Engineering, and science. No scientific credentials appear beside Mr. Benda's name in the company profiles of staff members.

Mr. Benda's connection with the tobacco industry has been documented since 1993 in a contract with Philip Morris to "perform services related to Strategic Technical Performance (STS)". The services for which Mr. Benda's company was paid $200,000 from October 31, 1993 to November 15, 1994 included submitting a paper to the American Society of Heating, Refrigerating and Air-conditioning Engineers (ASHRAE) for "cost effective methods of accommodation". Philip Morris refers to smoking being permitted as "accommodation".

In addition, should Mr. Benda be required to testify or present case studies, he would be paid an additional fee of $1,500.00 per day plus expenses. (13)

On August 12, 1994, the Chelsea Group sent a 180-page submission to the U.S. Dept. of Labor regarding "Occupational Safety and Health Association (OSHA) rules on indoor air quality. (14). This tobacco-funded submission claimed:

"The tobacco smoke requirements of the [OSHA] rule are economically and technically infeasible for application in restaurants, bars, bowling centres, night clubs and many other hospitality and entertainment venues. These facilities are oriented to providing service to customers who may or may not choose to smoke and will be severely impacted if the proposed requirements were mandated...in most facilities simple solutions to ventilation problems would result in a substantial reduction in ETS levels."

Obvious by its absence is the priority assigned to occupational health and safety of workers whose job descriptions should, according to Mr. Benda, include exposure to the toxic waste produced by lighted cigarettes.

In February 1997 Mr. Benda presented a submission claiming ventilation technology would accommodate both smokers and nonsmokers when a proposed clean indoor air ordinance was being considered in Honolulu, Hawaii. City Council voted on the ordinance and vacated all provisions covering restaurants. (15)

Tobacco manufacturers have good reason to worry about the improved standards of occupational health and safety which now extend to smoke-free bars and restaurants. A quadrupled quit rate in workplaces where smoking is no longer allowed means more lost business and threatened profits.

"Financial impact of smoking bans will be tremendous – Three to five fewer cigarettes per day per smoker will reduce annual manufacturer profits a billion dollars plus per year." National Smokers Alliance July, 1993 Bates Number 2025771934

National Smokers Alliance/Centre for Individual Freedom

"The National Smokers Alliance (NSA) is a not for profit membership organization dedicated to achieving a national policy that supports fair accomodation [sic] for smokers. The NSA represents the
views of a majority of Americans, smokers and non-smokers, who
believe fair accomodation [sic] is a reasonable alternative to government imposed bans. The NSA is working diligently to ensure
than those adults who chooses [sic] to smoke are not penalized by
excessive government regulation and higher taxes on tobacco products". (16)

When the tobacco cartel could no longer ignore the serious threat to
their profits persistently posed by health authorities, scientists, medical professionals and governments, they pooled their impressive financial resources to set up the National Smokers' Alliance, yet another
front group promoting tobacco's agenda. The NSA unswervingly re
sist any efforts to regulate the purchase and consumption of tobacco
products, claiming such measures to be in violation of smokers' personal liberties and illustrate un-necessary government interference
imposed on the lives of private citizens who make what is referred to
as in-your-face "politically incorrect" personal choices. Apparently
those who make a smoke-free choice do not enjoy the same personal
liberty or respect, because they are directed to "stay away if you don't
like the smoke". The NSA tolerates no discussion about negative health
consequences of smoking and exposure to secondhand smoke, claiming studies completed and peer reviewed by world class scientists have
"statistically insignificant" results which have been "skewed" by
"junkscientists" who are also "liars".

The NSA Board of Directors included Thomas Humber, the public
relations professional who had been managing the Philip Morris account for the public relations firm of Burson-Marstellar and two lawyers from Hunton & Williams, Philip Morris' law firm in the state of
Virginia.

Philip Morris directed $42 million to the National Smokers Alli-
ance between 1993 and 1996. The National Smokers Alliance, according to its tax returns, received $74,000 annually from membership dues
($10 per year from 7,400 members). Thomas Humber collected an
annual salary of $450,000 from the NSA in 1996 – six times the total

collected from membership fees.(17)

Boisterous talk show host Morton Downey (Mort the Mouth) had become notorious for blowing smoke in the faces of his guests who annoyed him. He claimed to have started smoking at age 11. In 1996, the National Smokers Alliance recruited him as their spokesperson. Following lung cancer surgery later that year, he called a press conference and exposed the National Smokers Alliance for what it was: just another tobacco front group. In his letter of resignation to the NSA, he said, "I am a person who is tragically addicted to smoking cigarettes and because of my public persona, am one of the most visible smokers in the country. Though I still defend the rights of people to smoke, I am no longer confident that the information imparted by the tobacco manufacturers and the NSA reflect the truth." (18) He taped public service announcements declaring he was an idiot for ever starting to smoke, and expressed his hope he could undo some of the damage he had caused for so many years on television by telling the truth, finally, about his false portrayal of smoking being a voluntary choice, because nicotine addiction removes any hope of free will.

Morton Downey died of lung cancer in March 2001.

The Centre for Individual Freedom (CIF) shares an address with the National Smokers Alliance in Alexandria, Virginia. Tax records filed by the CIF confirm three employees who also appear on the payroll of the National Smokers Alliance: William Thomas Humber (President), David Eric Schippers (Secretary) and David M. Nummy (Treasurer). In the identical period of time, William Thomas Humber was also CEO of the NSA; David Eric Schippers its Vice-President and David M. Nummy, its "Director as Needed".

On June 24, 1997, Walter Merryman, the Tobacco Institute Vice President was quoted as saying "All we're going to do is change the name on the door. We're going to continue to do what we've always done." (19)

On June 29, 1999 Philip Morris announced plans to withdraw its support from the National Smokers Alliance. Changing the name on their door did not even require moving offices.

"Tobacco industry reports on their (health) research are magnificent works of fiction ... When we put money in for research we put the research in straightjackets so that the people were limited how far they looked — and if they came beyond a certain point

which would reflect badly on the tobacco industry, it came to an end." Tony Van den Bergh, Former Tobacco executive Godfrey Phillips Tobacco Company (Britain) *Tobacco Wars,* Three part mini-series narrated by Walter Cronkite TLC & BBC News July/August 1999.

Whitecoat Project

Philip Morris could easily be nominated for doing more to obscure the truth about secondhand tobacco smoke than any other member of the tobacco cartel. Their virtually infinite financial resources paved the way for them to pay as much as would ever be required muddy the waters about health consequences of secondhand smoke exposure, concealing the secret and true agenda of protecting the interests of tobacco sales.

The déjà vu of tobacco industry efforts to keep controversy alive reappears in tobacco's unique brand of science. Its mandate remains consistent, and persistent: to dilute the results of many years of research by accredited scientists and medical doctors confirming secondhand smoke is as deadly, and in some situations, even worse than what a smoker voluntarily inhales. Nonsmokers involuntarily inhale tobacco smoke without benefit of filter tips smokers use as minimal protection from Class A carcinogens, heavy metals and hundreds of other poisons contained in cigarette smoke - many of which would not be allowed to be dumped in a sanitary landfill.

Secondhand smoke derives from two sources – the lighted end of a cigarette resting in an ashtray, or held by the smoker, and the smoke exhaled from a smoker (whose lungs have considerably filtered out some of the toxins and tar). Philip Morris, however, promoted their own brand of research, concluding that directly inhaling toxic waste into the lungs presented no significant health risk. Philip Morris seemed to be prepared to spend whatever would be required to make sure the public would hear this particular lie from contrived respectable sources. The tobacco industry coined the phrase "environmental tobacco smoke" when describing secondhand smoke, exploiting the use of the word "environmental" in their efforts to give the impression of unavoidable and grudgingly acceptable pollution.

The tobacco cartel had one remaining option to gain any degree of credibility in the scientific and medical communities: enticing medical and scientific professionals with seemingly disproportionately high remuneration to side with their views that no causal relationship exists between smoking and disease. Tobacco documents label tobacco-friendly scientists as "Independent Scientists" and "Whitecoats". These terms describe recruits in a multimillion dollar effort to discredit the growing quantity of accepted and peer-reviewed scientific research data confirming the health risks of involuntary, or passive smoking Whitecoat Project (20) strategy is clearly outlined in tobacco's confidential documents.

The mandate of the Whitecoat Project was fourfold: (21)

➢   Resist and roll back smoking restrictions.
➢   Restore smoker confidence.
➢   Reverse scientific and popular misconception that ETS is harmful.
➢   Restore social acceptability of smoking.

Beyond recruiting medical and scientific professionals loyal to tobacco interests, the tobacco cartel realized their voice must be heard in established and respected medical journals.

"Philip Morris presented to the UK industry their global strategy on environmental tobacco smoke. In every major international area (USA, Europe, Australia, Far East, South America, Central American and Spain) they are proposing, in key countries, to set up a team of scientists organized by one national coordinating scientist and American lawyers, to review scientific literature or carry out work on ETS to keep the controversy alive..." (22)

Philip Morris strategy to protect company interests and profit margins has always taken top priority. Telling the truth about what they do and how they do it apparently does not rate highly on the scale of importance. Operation Whitecoat was no exception. Seeing themselves cornered over irrefutable scientific research confirming the dangerous and lethal nature of the products they manufacture and sell, their retaliation had to be hard-hitting and front page. No details escaped their notice when planning their next move.

"...The [scientific] consultants should, ideally, according to Philip Morris, be European scientists who have had no previous connections with tobacco companies and who have no previous record on the primary [health] issue which might... lead to problems of attribution. The mechanism by which they identify their consultants is as follows: they ask a couple of scientists in each country...to produce a list of potential consultants. The scientists are then contacted by these coordinators or by the lawyers and asked if they are interested in problems of Indoor Air Quality: tobacco is not mentioned at this stage.

CV's are obtained and obvious "anti-smokers" or those with "unsuitable backgrounds" are filtered out..." (23)

Covington & Burling, Philip Morris' British law firm, would act as the executive arm of the operation, acting as *"legal buffer... the inter face with the operating units (whitecoats, laboratories, etc.)"*. (24) Tobacco attorneys prepared letters containing questionable claims about the "insignificant" and "unproven" health consequences of exposure to secondhand smoke. For a fee, scientists signed these letters and submitted them for publication to respected medical and scientific journals.

A Philip Morris memo from 1990 outlined *Whitecoat Project* and how scientists were recruited by tobacco, including a consultant who had published a book *Follies and Fallacies in Medicine*. This book was co-authored by Petr Skabanek and James McCormick. James McCormick, emeritus professor of community health at Trinity College, Dublin, claims he received no payment from Philip Morris. When asked if Petr Skabanek had ever been on Philip Morris' payroll, he replied "Petr may have done. I don't know. We both knew there were people in the tobacco industry . . . who thought our views were less inimical to their products than others." (25)

Petr Skabanek, an associate professor of community health at Trinity College in Dublin, regularly argued against disease prevention. He favored the notion of inevitability of diseases such as lung cancer, for which he maintained genetic predisposition prevailed as a factor for lung cancer moreso than the piffling aspect of smoking. Dr. Skabanek, a chain smoker, died of lung cancer in 1994 at the age of 53.

Gio Gori is a former scientist at the National Cancer Institute (U.S.) who sold his opinion for tobacco dollars. In a 1998 article in the Pioneer Press, David Hanning wrote that Dr. Gori was paid $20,137 for two letters to the Wall Street Journal, one letter to the British medical publication *The Lancet*, one letter to the *NCI Journal* and one opinion piece to the *Wall Street Journal*. (26)

Although the opinion piece was rejected by the editors of the *Wall Street Journal*, Gori sent his bill to the Philip Morris law firm of Covington and Burling for $4,137.50, for services rendered. (27)

Thirteen scientists were paid over $U.S.156,000.00 for letters and reports to discredit the Environmental Protection Agency data confirming secondhand smoke is a Class A carcinogen. (28) The obviously deliberate attempt to exaggerate the degree of dispute over health

consequences of exposure to tobacco smoke provides the common de-
nominator for the lawyer-prepared letters signed by science professionals who, evidence indicates, sold out to the highest bidder: tobacco.

The most respected journals became the targets of the tobacco industry in their desperate attempt for respectability in medicine and science. Over a six-month period in 1993, the *Journal of the National
Cancer Institute* (well known by Gori) published seven letters disput-
ing the negative consequences of tobacco smoke. Tobacco rewarded
their mouthpieces by paying them $US 28,550. (29)

Frank G. Colby, R. J. Reynolds Tobacco Company's Manager/Di-
rector of Scientific Information (1951-1979) and Associate Director of
Scientific Issues (1979-1983), had a clear mandate in his job description: "To efficiently provide the technical expertise necessary for the
Company to combat anti-tobacco claims". (30) Mr. Colby identified a
clear rating system for selection of tobacco-friendly appointments:

RATING DEFINITIONS:

1 = *Means the author...is more or less unequivocally on our side.*

2 = *Means that preponderance is given to etiological factors other
than smoking but that cigarettes smoking is mentioned as one among
many other etiological factors. In some cases it may mean that the
author is on our side for one group of diseases such as, for example,
cardiovascular diseases, even though he may be against us in other
areas such as, for example, respiratory cancers.*

3 = *Means that the author is more or less against us — i.e., he consid-
ers smoking the or a major etiological factor, but that there are other
factors which more or less mitigate this correlation. (31)*

He rated scientific submissions as they related to the tobacco agenda
from a 1 ("all favorable") to a minus 3 ("foaming at the mouth").

**"...they [Philip Morris] are proposing, in key countries, to set
up a team of scientists organized by one national coordinating scientist and American lawyers, to review scientific literature or carry
out work on ETS to keep the controversy alive. They are spending
vast sums of money..."**

**"The scientists are then contacted by these coordinators or by
the lawyers and asked if they are interested in problems of Indoor
Air Quality: tobacco is not mentioned at this stage. CVs are obtained and obvious 'anti-smokers' or those with 'unsuitable backgrounds' are filtered out.**

17 February 1988, *Note on a special meeting of the UK Industry on Environmental Tobacco Smoke,* **BAT 301150179-184**

The tobacco industry continued to buy and pay for attacks against respected sources of scientific data confirming each time the alarming extent of devastation caused to global public health as a result of smoking, both from active smoking and from exposure to secondhand smoke became known. The World Health Organization has declared war on the tobacco industry. When tobacco can no longer refute scientific data, their next strategy historically is to dismantle and discredit the source of any information damaging to their interests.

Robert Tollison and Richard Wagner were commissioned by the tobacco industry to write their report criticizing the World Health Organization, in which they clearly overstated the WHO's Tobacco or Health budget. They claimed the budget for this totalled $US 11,884,300 for the two years 1994 and 1995 and were scathing in their opinions on the vast resources wasted on attempting tobacco control. (32) The actual budget for the years 1994 and 1995 for the Tobacco or Health WHO project was not $US 11,884,300. It was US$ 1,884,300, ten million dollars less than Tollison and Wagner reported in their paper. OOPS!!! A mere ten million dollar discrepancy! Could that have been an "innocent" mistake? A "typo" that escaped proofreaders?

Since this report was widely circulated to the world press to inflame outrage over mismanagement of funds by the World Health Organization, any disclaimers acknowledging the "mistake" appeared too late to be noticed. The inflated and inaccurate figure continued to appear for years in tobacco-instigated reports criticizing the World Health Organization. In the words of Neil Collishaw, currently the Research Director with Physicians for a Smoke-Free Canada and former lead tobacco control expert for the World Health Organization in Geneva at the time,

"Just to get at the Tobacco or Health Program they were ready to destroy the credibility of the world's leading public health agency. A military strategist would admire the tobacco industry tactics for that one. If you want to win, shoot the guy out front." (33)

"We anticipate that if Repace runs true to form there will be a good deal of media copy written about their analysis and thus we should begin eroding confidence in this work as soon as possible."

February 25, 1985 letter by Dr. Anthony Colucci, (RJR Scientist)
Wall Street Journal **April 28, 1998**

Tobacco-Funded "Think Tanks" and Additional Front Groups

Big Tobacco donate generously to what are known as libertarian think–
tanks, a term translating into tobacco support. Hidden patronage of
this type maintains controversy about the health consequences of smoking and exposure to secondhand smoke. "Researchers" with little or
no medical or scientific training regularly accuse health professionals
of providing false research conclusions and do an impressive job of
number crunching, themselves, to "prove" that no foundation exists to
any notion about smoking making anyone sick. The condescending
and uneducated conclusion of all such reports remains consistent – no
need for anti-tobacco hysteria, because smoking has never been proven
to cause illness.

A further report in the San Francisco Chronicle states that the conservative think tanks received $3.5 million from the drug and tobacco
industries to protest and challenge Federal Drug Administration (FDA)
regulatory processes. The FDA have been attempting to regulate tobacco products for years . (34)

The publication *"Lies, Damned Lies and 400,000 Smoking Related
Deaths"* appeared in the Fall 1998 issue of *Regulation* (The Cato Review of Business and Government), co-authored by Rosalind Marimont
and Robert Levy. Rosalind Marimont lists her credentials as being a
"mathematician and scientist" but does not specify her discipline of science has been confined to the realm of digital computers. (35) Robert
Levy teaches statistics to lawyers at Georgetown Law Centre. (36) Neither has any formal training in medicine or medical science. Both have a
forte with numbers and use this well in a transparent and unsuccessful
attempt to discredit research from their scientific superiors.

The Fraser Institute

The tobacco industry also call in favors for their financial support through
the Fraser Institute by way of regularly published predictable attacks on
scientific data confirming the negative health consequences of tobacco
use. In 1999 the book *"Passive Smoke – the EPA Betrayal of Science and
Policy"* arrived, with a price tag of $20. The price was waived, however,

for those free copies distributed to public officials throughout North America. This book was co-authored by Gio Gori and John Luik in support of tobacco-lobbying judge Osteen's decision to vacate part of the EPA report identifying secondhand smoke as a Class A carcinogen. Gio Gori accepted payment to sign letters prepared by tobacco lawyers for submission to medical journals and John Luik lied about having completed his doctoral studies before he actually did. (37) (38) Gio Gori and John Luik represent the tobacco cartel well.

Associates for Research in Substance Enjoyment ("ARISE")

Burson Marstellar, longtime public relations firm on Philip Morris' payroll, enacted the first of many strategies in their attempts to reverse the increasing rejection of smoking as an integral aspect of socializing. An allegedly dispassionate group of scientific professionals assembled to voice an allegedly independent opinion embracing "substance enjoyment". The substances mentioned included tea, coffee, alcohol, chocolate, gourmet food - oh, and don't forget - tobacco. Slip it in and say it quickly before anyone notices the attempt to equate nicotine addiction with enjoyment of a chocolate or a good cuppa. Press conferences and meetings promoted guilt-free enjoyment of a full life , apparently incomplete without gratifying nicotine withdrawal at regular intervals.

   "Yolande de la Bigne, a well-known [French] journalist, covered the [ARISE Paris] conference...concluding that 'a piece of chocolate, a glass of wine, a good cigarette, you can go for it. Instead of being obsessed by health, everybody should be obsessed by pleasure which induces good health. Le Parisien also covered the conference in a lengthy feature entitled 'Pleasure is good medicine'." (39)

   ARISE and Yolande de la Bigne classify gratifying nicotine withdrawal in the same category as drinking tea and coffee, eating food, and indulging in bars of chocolate. They do not, however, offer any numbers to illustrate how many die from eating or consuming tea/coffee/chocolate to compare with the 400,000 who die annually in the U.S. from smoking.

The Advancement of Sound Science Coalition (TASSC)

Philip Morris' 1954 budget included $880,000 funding for TASSC. On

advice from their P.R. company (Burston Marsellar), and following a
$50,000 "feasibility study", strategy to set up a European parallel be-
gan. Protests against smoking issues buried themselves deeply beneath
a variety of unrelated tobacco controversies such as pesticide restrictions, use of bovine growth hormones and regulations on the use of
chlorine. (40) The Advancement of Sound Science Coalition's true
mandate left no doubt when discussed in secret documents: *"Associate anti-industry "scientific" studies with broader questions about
government research and regulation. Link tobacco use with other
more "politically correct" products."* (41)

TASSC operated with a skeleton staff from the same address as APCO.
In compliance with instructions from its tobacco benefactors, TASSC
did not restrict its criticism of the Environmental Protection Agency and
the World Health Organization to tobacco issues. It also received funding from 3M, Dow, Exxon and Procter & Gamble and regularly demanded
"sound science" while claiming global warming is a "farce", downplaying
pesticides in baby food and shrugging off the consequences of involuntary exposure to tobacco smoke. Soon after a 1998 story appeared in the
New York Times exposing their extensive corporate funding, TASSC
faded out as suddenly as it had arrived. (42)

**"In Canada, we orchestrated a national media tour by the U.K.
leader of the Freedom Organization for the Right to Enjoy Smoking Tobacco (FOREST), which generated a large amount of favorable media coverage and led to the creation of a Canadian counterpart, Smokers Freedom Society." Philip Morris Inter-Office
Correspondence , to Board of Directors from Andrew Whist, December 17, 1986 Bates Number 2025431401. The "Smokers Freedom Society" received initial funding of $100,000 from the Cana-
dian Tobacco Industry (*"Pro-smokers' group founded with help from
tobacco firms*," p. D1, Montreal *Gazette*, Sept. 4th, 1986)**

International Agency for Research on Cancer (IARC) (43)

Within the framework of tobacco industry misinformation achieve-
ments, top prize goes to their expensive and extensive effort to dismantle the   greatest threat to their interests, a seven-year European
research project which demonstrated that passive smokers faced a 16
per cent increase in the relative risk of lung cancer. The cost of the

WHO/IARC research totalled US$2 million over a seven year period. Philip Morris allocated US$6 million over two years to do whatever was required to infiltrate the scientific team, monitor the work at each stage of completion and dilute the conclusions with deliberately "leaked" inaccurate press releases. (44)

Conrad Black, a Canadian media tycoon, is also Chairman and C.E.O. of Hollinger Inc., the third largest newspaper chain in the world which owns (among others) the London Telegraph. Conrad Black's editorial policy was reported in *Maclean's* (45) when Conrad Black told his staff:

"If editors disagree with us they should disagree with us when they're no longer in our employ. The buck stops with ownership. I am responsible for meeting the payroll; therefore I will ultimately determine what the papers say and how they're going to be run."

Conrad Black's wife, Canadian journalist Barbara Amiel, served as a trustee for the partially tobacco-funded Fraser Institute in Vancouver. (46)

On Sunday, March 8, 1998, the London Sunday Telegraph headline proclaimed "Passive Smoking Doesn't Cause Cancer – Official". (47) The story unfolded with the clear implication that the World Health Organization withheld information for publication from its own seven-year study because the research had failed to prove causal association between smoking and lung cancer.

In fact, the conclusions from the WHO/IARC research supported previous research confirming exposure to secondhand smoke does indeed cause lung cancer. The report had not yet been made public because in accordance with standard procedure, it had been submitted for peer review. The tobacco industry had deliberately planted an erroneous story on the front page of a leading British newspaper (which happens to be owned by a tobacco sympathizer). On Monday March 9, 1998 a press release was issued by the World Health Organization. (48)

"The World Health Organization (WHO) has been publicly accused of suppressing information. Its opponents say that WHO has withheld from publication its own report that was aimed at but supposedly failed to scientifically prove that there is an association between passive smoking, or environmental tobacco smoke (ETS), and a number of diseases, lung cancer in particular. Both statements are untrue.

The study in question is a case-control study on the effects of ETS on lung cancer risk in European populations, which has been carried out over the last seven years by 12 research centres in 7 European countries under the leadership of WHO's cancer research branch — the International Agency for Research on Cancer (IARC).

The results of this study, which have been completely misrepresented in recent news reports, are very much in line with the results of similar studies both in Europe and elsewhere: passive smoking causes lung cancer in non-smokers.

The study found that there was an estimated 16% increased risk of lung cancer among non-smoking spouses of smokers. For workplace exposure the estimated increase in risk was 17%. However, due to small sample size, neither increased risk was statistically significant. Although, the study points towards a decreasing risk after cessation of exposure.

In February 1998, according to usual scientific practice, a paper reporting the main study results was sent to a reputable scientific journal for consideration and peer review. That is why the full report is not yet publicly available. Under the circumstances, however, the authors of the study have agreed to make an abstract of the report available to the media.

"It is extremely important to note that the results of this study are consistent with the results of major scientific reviews of this question published during 1997 by the government of Australia, the US Environmental Protection Agency and the State of California", said Neil Collishaw, Acting Chief of WHO's Tobacco or Health Unit in Geneva. "A major meta-analysis of passive smoking and lung cancer was also published in the British Medical Journal in 1997. From these and other previous reviews of the scientific evidence emerges a clear global scientific consensus — passive smoking does cause lung cancer and other diseases", he concluded.

"IARC is proud of the careful scientific work done by the European scientific team responsible for this study", commented Dr Paul Kleihues, the Agency's director. "We are very concerned about the false and misleading statements recently published in the mass media. It is no coincidence that this misinformation originally appeared in the British press just before the No-Tobacco Day in the United Kingdom and the scheduled publication of the report of the British Scientific Committee on Tobacco and Health".

The monkey wrench had landed squarely at its intended destination: right in the middle of the research division of the biggest health agency in the world. No retraction ever appeared in the London Telegraph to explain the misinformation behind its original headline claiming the inaccurate "official" conclusion of the World Health Organization that passive smoke does not cause lung cancer. The WHO press release never appeared in the London Telegraph.

Conrad Black is the Canadian media mogul some compare with Australia's Rupert Murdoch. Rupert Murdoch is on the Board of Directors of Philip Morris and the Cato Institute. (49) (50) In 1998 Geoffrey Bible, CEO of Philip Morris, was voted on to the board of Rupert Murdoch's News Corp., one of the world's most powerful media and entertainment companies, an event that passed, unsurprisingly, with minimal news coverage. (51) Rupert Murdoch's News Corp owns Harper Collins publishing, TV Guide, the New York Post in addition to 20th Century Fox and Fox Broadcasting. Among other holdings are TV stations in New York, Washington, Los Angeles, Philadelphia, Chicago, Atlanta, Boston, Phoenix and 14 other cities. They possess the power to disclose – or not – whatever information they choose relating to tobacco interests.

"We are in a nicotine rather than a tobacco industry ...After the presentation, the group had a discussion on the organoleptic effects of nicotine....Another easy test of free nicotine odor and irritation involves smelling some as it is eluted from a gas chromatograph — a small amount will almost knock one over and the aroma is apparent." Project "Mad Hatter" designed to minimize harmful effects of tobacco smoke exposure 1971   Bates No. 682012257/2258

Light Cigarettes - The Scam

Desperately seeking acceptance, tobacco advocates claim so-called "low tar" "mild", "ultra light" and "light" cigarettes provide the alleged adult pleasure of smoking, without the inconvenient side-effect of inhaling a quart of tar a year into the lungs, delivered by consumption of regular cigarettes for the pack a day smoker. (52)

For cigarettes to qualify as "light" or "low tar", results from testing of tar and nicotine levels in government laboratories must fall below those of regular cigarettes. To circumvent laboratory smoking machine results, "light" cigarettes contain microscopic laser perforations in the filter tips which facilitate significant quantities of smoke to escape the notice of the smoking machines registering levels of tar and nicotine. (53) Smoking machines do not have human lips, which in reality block the escape of tar and nicotine when a real human smokes a cigarette. Tobacco documents discuss "flow rates" (54) and scientists observe how smokers seen to be adjusting to lower delivery. (55) No tobacco scientist seems to know or care about the "adjustments" smokers of lower nicotine cigarettes must make to obtain an equivalent buzz of nicotine: they inhale more deeply, and smoke more cigarettes. This results in yet another lung cancer caused by smoking, known as adeno-carcinoma. (56) (57)

Doctoral researchers a Penn State analyzed 158 discarded butts from so-called "light" cigarettes and found the microscopic vent holes on the "light" and "ultra light" brands most often circle a cigarette's filter one half inch from the tip, a carefully engineered distance to correspond to the blocking of these holes with smokers' lips and fingertips. (58)

One Philip Morris document from 1975 says, for example, *"Marlboro Lights were not smoked like regular Marlboros. In effect, the Marlboro 85 [a full-strength brand] smokers in this study did not achieve any reduction in smoke intake by smoking a [Marlboro Light] cigarette."* (59)

In June 2001, Alan Rock, the Canadian Minister of Health issued a deadline of three months to the tobacco industry to remove the terms mild and light from their cigarette packaging. Predictably Imperial Tobacco responded with protests their customers would be "confused" and denied they ever made claims that light and mild claims about their products implied any notion such products were less dangerous than "regular" cigarettes. Early in 2002, Canadian cigarette manufac-turers issued a press release to say they were "voluntarily removing" the words *mild* and *light* from their package labelling.

"We would very much like R.J. Reynolds to inform the consumer that the product is, in fact, contaminated with glass fibres." John Pauly, PhD, Dept. of Immunology at Roswell Park Cancer Insti-tute, Buffalo New York, referring to "Eclipse" cigarettes pro-claimed by R.J. Reynolds Tobacco to be smoke-free and safer *Less Deadly Cigarettes : Lesser Evil or Dangerous Alternative?* April, 2000

Eclipse – The "SAFE" cigarette

Eclipse: to obscure; darken; To diminish in importance, fame, or reputation.

The dictionary definition of *eclipse* provides an accurate description of how tobacco has been promoted, the only consumer product allowed on the market without full disclosure of side effects and health risks. This also happens to be the name of an alleged "safer" cigarette.

Eclipse cigarettes don't actually burn and therefore do not produce smoke. From that aspect they appear to be safer because nonsmokers are not exposed to the toxic waste produced from the end of regular cigarettes. The charcoal filter tip is placed in the mouth and the cigarette is set on fire, heating (not burning) the tobacco via a carbon fuel rod which generates an aerosol with a nicotine and tobacco flavor. This carbon fuel rod in *Eclipse* cigarettes is insulated and bound in two wrappings of glass fibers, found throughout 95% of the cigarettes. (60)

Contrary to RJR's public reassurance, documents from RJR confirm they know carcinogenic glass fibres are released from *Eclipse* filters during smoking, and inhaled.

Unsurprisingly, RJR declared the glass fibers were "too big to be inhaled". Of course, an industry whose product when used as directed has killed millions expects to be obeyed and believed in all things. Don't they?

Eclipse reduces secondhand smoke by 90% - good news for non-smokers. Trouble is, nicotine delivery to the smoker is also reduced. A smoker's priority will always be nicotine, not secondhand smoke. *Eclipse* cigarettes arrived to address public concern about secondhand smoke. Unable to make health claims about their product, R. J. Reynolds said this product "appeared to be safer" than conventional cigarettes, based on the results of mouse-painting tests (animal lovers, avert your eyes for the next part).

Mouse-painting tests are conducted by the tobacco industry, who paint a test solution of nicotine and tar directly on mice's skin, who are then observed for "adverse reactions" (a.k.a. tumor growth). Mice painted with residue from *Eclipse* cigarettes showed no evidence of developing tumors while mice coated with the residue from conventional low-tar cigarettes developed tumors in 24 of 40 cases.

RJ Reynolds spokesman, Seth Moskowitz futilely attempted to diminish ("eclipse"?) any notion that normal cigarettes are dangerous by saying: "There have been studies available since the '50s that show skin-painting of tar produces tumors. But what relevance does that have to inhalation of cigarette smoke?" - thereby ignoring the reason why tobacco scientists perform this cruel experiment on mice and the parallel reality of the consequences of tar delivery to delicate lung tissue – ten times with each cigarette. (61)

Science and medical professionals don't see it that way. Why have the American Lung Society called for removal of *Eclipse* from the market? (62) Why have one group of scientists declared it more dangerous than regular cigarettes? You can be forgiven for the déjà vu you're probably experiencing; remember "low tar" cigarettes?

Maybe it will take a court of law to ensure, again, the manufacturers of tobacco products disclose all they know. In the meantime, tobacco bank (literally) on the prospect of profits exceeding any future settlements they will have to pay. They epitomize the cliché that it is easier to make amends than it is to get permission.

As for *Eclipse*?   In ancient times, eclipses were superstitiously regarded as forerunners of evil fortune.   Some things never change.

Ammonia chemistry – Maximize Nicotine 'Hit'

"An alternative approach is to treat the tobacco, which has its nicotine naturally tied up in the form of nicotine salts, with a stronger base than nicotine, such as ammonia." The free nicotine in smoke would have a much greater physiological effect than nicotine salts." Lorillard *"Nicotine Augmentation Project"*, H.J. Minnemeyer to Dr. F.J. Schultz May 4, 1976

The acrid odor of ammonia is familiar to most people. It is used in hair dyes, cleaning solutions, fertilizers and explosives. Less than a whiff can cause respiratory distress . Contact with the eyes can result in blindness and OSHA directives indicate the affected individual must not be near open flame. Ammonia burns the skin.

Ammonia and ammonia compounds also effectively convert, equilibrate and change nicotine from salt into a free base. Like cocaine, nicotine exists in two forms – acid and base. When ammonia is added, nicotine converts from acid to base form. The base form can vaporize more easily from smoke particles into the gas phase, facilitating it to deposit directly on to lung tissue, and immediately diffuse through the body. Hi-tech SPECT and PET brain scans confirm nicotine takes six to seven seconds to "hit" the brain, and release the dopamine rush producing the feel-good sensation smokers refer to as "relaxing". (63) This is one half the time required for injected heroin to affect brain chemistry and produce the rush of dopamine smokers describe as pleasurable. (64)

"PM is also using ammonium carbonate to facilitate nicotine release in denicotinizing tobacco for their new "de-nic" brands. These all seem to use the same 100% fluo-cured blend, but blend ends up with twice the ammonia level of their Marlboro blend."

"AMMONIA AS IMPACT BOOSTER"

Ammonia, when added to a tobacco blend, reacts with the indigenous nicotine salts and liberates free nicotine. As a result of such change, the ratio of extractable nicotine to bound nicotine in the smoke may be altered in favor of extractable nicotine. As we know, extractable nicotine contributes to impact in cigarette smoke and this is how ammonia can act as an impact booster." "A cigarette incorporating RT will deliver more flavor compounds, including nicotine, into smoke than one without it."

(RT= root technology, a euphemism for engineering tobacco plant growth to produce increased ammonia content)

"In the early 1950's, Philip Morris (PM) was also developing a band-cast recon [reconstituted tobacco – sweepings and 'leftovers' mixed and baked in sheets] *to realize the economies of fully using stems and tobacco fines. Pectin release was accomplished by cooking the slurry with DAP (diammonium phosphate, a nitrogen fertilizer) and adding more ammonia as necessary to maintain efficient pectin releasing conditions."*

"Ammonia is extremely volatile and is a gas at room temperature (boiling point 33.4 C). Therefore, if added as ammonia, per se, it would be lost from the tobacco quickly. The secret to using RT is to use it in the form of more stable compounds such as DAP or UREA, where heat will trigger the release of ammonia. A better approach is through prior reaction with tobacco such that ammonia can remain "bonded" through chemical reactions and be released by the action of heat." (65)

"Project Coumarin" Rat Poison Added to Pipe Tobacco (66)

Coumarin is a rat poison used in pipe tobacco to reduce the harsh stench of burning tobacco and "enhance" its "scent". Coumarin had been removed from cigarettes following the FDA ruling which prohibited the use of coumarin in foods with additives. This ruling did not extend to pipe tobacco, and coumarin remains in use.

"The National Council on Smoking and Health <u>does not know</u> [sic] that coumarin is used in some types of cigarettes but has heard of the substance. The Chairman of the Council, Mr. Snell Bartveit states, however, that the Council last year sent a query in writing to the Directorate of Public Health, requesting that the problems surrounding the use of additives on a <u>general</u> [sic] basis be taken up with the tobacco industry."

"So far, the joint body of the industry has replied by referring to practice abroad – that the question of additives is a business/production secret which will not be answered."

"As coumarin is a substance which, according to Norwegian experts, stimulates the heart and has a cancer-inducing effect, a focusing on it would be likely to attract a considerable publicity."

"In the Directorate of Public Health, work on the problems surrounding additives is given very low priority, and this will delay the process. The tobacco industry will initially not disclose to the Directorate of Public Health, the use of additives used in tobacco, if approached." (67)

The tobacco industry claim that coumarin is a "natural" product, a derivative of the tonka bean which produces scented seeds used as a vanilla substitute. In 1954 the Food and Drug Administration banned coumarin as a food additive based on rodent studies that coumarin instigated liver toxicity. Banned as a food additive, coumarin continues to be used as a scent fixative and enhancing agent in soaps, detergents and cosmetic preparations.

The tobacco industry continue to add coumarin to their pipe tobacco to mask its natural putrid stench. In 1992 the National Toxicology Program confirmed coumarin to be a lung specific carcinogen, and required tobacco companies to report cigarette additives to the U. S. Department of Health and Human Services. (68) No such requirement has ever been imposed for pipe tobacco. The FDA's "GRAS" (Generally Recognized As Safe) list has not included coumarin for many years.

*"The tobacco companies have released their own safety assess-
ment of additives, noting that "approximately 98% of all ingredients
... are approved as food additives by the FDA or have been given the
GRAS status, adding that "many of the ingredients are identical or
essentially similar in composition to natural leaf tobacco compo-
nents." The remaining 2% of the list, however, leaves approximately
80 ingredients which have not been approved. The report said the 28
ingredients present at the highest levels in cigarettes occur at levels
ranging from 0.05% to 9.28% by weight, the latter being sugars. The
remaining ingredients occur at levels below 500 ppm, and over one-
third occur at levels below 1 ppm. The industry's report states, "Based
upon analyses of all the toxicological data reviewed by the authors, it
was concluded that there was no evidence that any ingredient added
to cigarette tobacco produces harmful effects under the conditions
of use in cigarettes."* (69)

Note the absence of any mention of pipe tobacco.

**"You can SEE the proof of Kent's health protection! Exclusive
"Micronite" Filter removes 7 times more nicotine and tars ...and
you can see and taste the difference! Stop to think...and you'll start
to smoke KENT!" 1952 Kent cigarette advertisement. Micronite
filters contained crocidolite asbestos, responsible for malignant mesothelioma which affects the pleura (the sac lining the chest) and
the abdomen.**

Asbestos filter "proof of greather health protection"

Early advertising claims for the "micronite" filter manufactured in
Kent cigarettes included bogus endorsements from the American Medical Association. (70) Lorillard touted this revolutionary new filter tip
as a development of "researchers in atomic energy plants", and claimed
it removed seven times more tar and nicotine than any other brand.
Following protests and complaints from the American Medical Association, reference to their endorsement of this filter tip ceased; however, advertisements including models dressed as doctors reporting
ersatz scientific research brazenly claimed the safety and effectiveness
of this allegedly ground-breaking invention which protected smokers,
in an attempt to provide medical sanctions for their cigarettes.

Lorillard Tobacco's Idea of Health Protection for Sensitive Smokers was a lethal asbestos filter tip referred to as "micronite". Thirteen billion cigarettes with crocidolite asbestos filters were sold to millions of trusting smokers from 1952 - 1956.

In 1954, Lorillard had commissioned two separate studies using electron microscopes to prove that no harmful fibers were entering smokers' lungs. Both studies confirmed the opposite. The first two puffs through the micronite filter released 3.4 million crocidolite structures (clumps of fibers). (71) (72) A pack a day smoker of Kents inhaled 1.242 billion such structures over a twelve-month period of time. Thirteen **billion** cigarettes with crocidolite asbestos filters were sold to millions of trusting smokers over four years.

In May, 2000 a jury found Lorillard Tobacco guilty of negligence and product liability because from 1952 – 1956, Lorillard manufactured, marketed and sold Kent cigarettes with a "micronite" filter. $1,048,100.00 was awarded to the two children of a woman who died from malignant abdominal mesothelioma from smoking Kent cigarettes with "micronite" filters. Hailed in advertising as *"No other cigarette approaches such a degree of health protection and taste satisfaction"*, (73) the micronite filter contained crocidolite asbestos, the most dangerous carcinogenic of all asbestos filter types. Lorillard manufactured and sold cigarettes with this type of filter for two years following independent research they commissioned, results of which confirmed dangerous and potentially lethal fibre release from their "micronite" filter tips. By a jury vote of 9-3, Lorillard Tobacco Company was found to have committed oppression in its conduct. (74)

At the same time Lorillard knew Kent cigarettes "micronite" filter tips contained the most deadly kind of asbestos, Kents were advertised as a cigarette whose manufacturer went to the extra expense to protect smokers with "microscopic filtering".

Tobacco Judge, Wannabe Scientist

In 1974 Judge William Osteen was hired as a private lawyer by a group of private tobacco growers in three districts to represent them in Washington. He accepted payment to travel to Washington to fulfill his mandate of urging the U.S. Secretary of Agriculture not to proceed with a proposal to eradicate federal tobacco production control. (75)

In 1995 he allowed the tobacco cartel to file a suit challenging the EPA's research confirming that secondhand smoke is a Class A Carcinogen (a known carcinogen). Is it any coincidence that this challenge was filed in tobacco-friendly North Carolina, the seat of Judge Osteen's jurisdiction?

Canon 2A of the Code of Conduct for United States Judges clearly states: "A judge must avoid all impropriety and appearance of impropriety. The test for appearance of impropriety is whether the conduct would create in reasonable minds…a perception that the judge's ability to carry out judicial responsibilities with…impartiality…is impaired." (76)

The only chapters of the Environmental Protection Agency research set aside by judge Osteen were the most damaging to tobacco interests: those identifying secondhand smoke as a known carcinogen. The rest of the report confirming the negative health consequences of exposure to secondhand smoke remains intact, and includes: Acute respiratory illnesses in children; Acute and chronic middle ear diseases; Cough, phlegm and wheezing; asthma; Sudden Infant Death Syndrome; lung function in children; and respiratory symptoms and lung function in adults. The EPA's formal assessment of the increased risk for respiratory illnesses in children from secondhand smoke (contained in chapter eight of the EPA's report) was not vacated. (77)

Judge Osteen has a public record of pro tobacco advocacy, and he did not recuse himself from a high profile challenge critical to the future of tobacco interests. Judge Osteen ruled against the peer-reviewed and approved conclusions of a team of eighteen world-class scientists who agreed on the proven carcinogenic qualities of secondhand smoke.

Judge Osteen's decision has been under appeal since 1998. (78)

Summary

One thing can be said for the tobacco industry research scientists: they are the experts on addiction. Nobody understands better than they do the power of nicotine addiction over their customers, whose tobacco dependency guarantees repeat business until they either die, or manage to stop smoking.

Tobacco is chemically treated with ammonia to maximize the impact each puff of smoke makes on the human brain. The tobacco industry have collaborated to unite when necessary to speak with one voice and organize their own conspiracy to deceive their customers, the public and health authorities around the world.

Tobacco funded "experts" spare no expense to conduct "research" inevitably clouding established health issues and attempting to maintain controversy. Sell-out scientists and doctors who place a higher value on juicy cheques than their scientific integrity can be recruited to sign their names to tobacco-attorney prepared letters to editors of respected medical journals.

Front groups abound, shifting the focus at all times away from the known health consequences of smoking and towards issues alleging violation of civil liberties only for smokers, however. Those who choose to be smoke-free apparently don't count.

The innocuous-sounding vanilla bean produces a substance known to be a lung specific carcinogen, added to pipe tobacco whose only natural quality is the sickening stink when it is set on fire. To comply with public demand for a smokeless nicotine delivery device, an alternative cigarette hit the market, carefully constructed with fiberglass filaments whose ultimate destination will be the lung tissue of smokers.

When the largest environmental protection agency in the world completed its diligent and peer-reviewed research damning secondhand smoke as the Class A Carcinogen it is, tobacco made sure their appeal took place in a tobacco-friendly place under the auspices of a known tobacco friendly judge.

Big Tobacco and their loyal mouthpieces: the same people who call the World Health Organization "junkscientists".

"For more than 40 years the tobacco industry has known that the nicotine in cigarettes is addictive. Internally, the companies have long recognized that nicotine addiction is the prime reason that people continue to smoke. Publicly the companies have denied this, or, more recently, tried to fudge the definition of addiction. The industry maintains, however, that it has never been deceitful on the issue of nicotine and addiction: "We have not concealed, we do not conceal, and we will never conceal….We have no internal research which proves that smoking…is addictive."
T. Stevenson, BAT, Denies Smoking Claims, The Independent, 31 October 1996.

by kind permission of The QuitSmoking Co.

• IV - TOBACCO BRAND OF SILENCE •
Why Tell The Truth When Lies Sound Better?

"The cruelest lies are often told in silence." (Robert Louis Stevenson)

Robert Louis Stevenson's observation about the dark side of silence describes the less commonly considered brand of fraud favored by the tobacco industry: saying nothing. Quietly and behind closed doors, subversive tobacco activities relentlessly continue, protected by fiercely guarded secrecy. Silenced by very clear legislation to restrict advertising and sponsorship in the western world, the tobacco industry has shifted into high gear efforts to advertise its deadly product in countries whose governments place a lower priority on telling the truth than on collecting revenue.

Tobacco Differences: Developed, Underdeveloped and Developing Worlds

Although the incidence of smoking in developing countries is up to triple the rate in the developed world, the frequency of smoking deaths in developing countries lags behind, mostly due to other causes of death overtaking the smoking population before tobacco-related disease has the opportunity to manifest. (1) Sub-optimal medical care and facilities result in a high rate of death at a young age from infectious disease, whereas tar-coated lungs and oral cancer can take many years to make their presence known. The per capita rates of smoking have begun to reverse the existing trend. According to the Asian Consultancy on Tobacco Control, smoking decreases annually in the West by 1.1%, and increases by 2.1% annually in developing countries. (2)

The possibility of all those pink lungs belonging to potential smokers and the three hundred million existing smokers in China prompted tobacco executive Ibison D. Rothman of the Rothman International Tobacco Co. to joke **"Thinking about Chinese smoking statistics is like trying to think about the limits of space"**. (3)

As a country, China leads the world in cigarette consumption. Poland, however, maintains the highest per capita cigarette consumption of 3,620 cigarettes per year (compare to 2,590 in the West). (4) Predictably, increasing death rates from smoking diseases accompany the alarming rise in tobacco consumption. The devastating health consequences of tobacco use recognize no political boundary.

Increased prosperity in Korea translates into higher cigarette consumption. Although 60% - 80% of Korean men smoke, during more impoverished times and minimal disposable income, they could only afford to smoke one to two cigarettes daily. With reduced unemployment and higher wages arrives the ability to afford one to two *packs* of cigarettes daily. (5)

Tobacco magnates adapt well to compensate for the significant dent in their profit margins resulting from North American smoking restrictions. Indigent countries whose governments can be enticed by multi million dollar investment in factories and employment have become the focus of attention. The prospect of country coffers filled abundantly and reliably with revenue collected from tobacco sales persuades corrupt leaders to turn a blind eye to the promotion of tobacco, the only consumer product known for its ability to kill and maim its users.

Kenneth Clarke, British Member of Parliament for Rushcliffe (Nottinghamshire) wielded his influence during his June 2001 visit to Vietnam to promote the product of his tobacco mentors who want a piece of the lucrative pie in a country with the highest rate of smokers in the world. Kenneth Clark receives £100,000 a year as Deputy Chairman of British American Tobacco Company , and has been considered to serve them better than the voters who elected him to public office. He missed a state opening of Parliament to attend the BATCO annual Southeast Asia board meeting. Cloaked in predictable silence, Mr. Clarke and BATCO refuse to discuss their attempts to obtain government approval for the $40 million tobacco production plant with the Vietnamese tobacco company Vintaba. (6)

Tobacco's silent strategy includes securing a foot in the door to resist inevitable protests against expansion of tobacco influence.(7) Emphasis on a manufacturing facility providing jobs and guaranteeing government revenue for the next fifty years provides significant leverage against anyone who challenges the wisdom of reaping financial profits from a product that, according to the World Health Organization, will claim the lives of 10% of 7.3 million Vietnamese smokers.

"If multinational tobacco companies could capture the China market, it wouldn't make a difference if every American stopped smoking tomorrow." Dr. Judith Mackay, Hong Kong physician *Smok-*

ing Deaths Predicted to Triple, Philadelphia Inquirer **Jennifer Lin August 1997**

Get on board, little children, There's room for many a more.

These anonymous lyrics of a hymn describe the tobacco cartel's approach to global youth. Five empty cigarette packs (three, if you are a student) constitute the price of admission to rock concerts in Taipei, Taiwan and Novisibirsk, Siberia .(8) The Canton Disco in China allows distribution of free cigarettes, courtesy of R. J. Reynolds who also pay for entertainment.(9) Philip Morris sponsors a popular Beijing radio program The Marlboro American Music Hour (10).

No longer able to entice children with the prospect of early experimentation with "adult" behaviour in western countries, the tobacco cartel miss no opportunity to exploit impressionable youth where advertising standards have no obligation to disclose warnings about lack of product safety or provide consumer awareness. In deprived parts of the world where teenagers can only dream of escaping poverty and ignorance, smiling, smarmy models dressed as American cowgirls give away free cigarettes, Joe Camel logo toys, Marlboro Man tee shirts, baseball hats and CD's . Believing the hollow promises of tobacco that smoking transforms poverty into affluence, awkwardness into sophistication and immaturity into adult wisdom, children choose to experiment with smoking cigarettes. They do not choose drug addiction. By the time they realize nicotine has turned them into addicts, the silence of deception has won another victory and removed any possibility of free choice.

No limits exist on tobacco billboard advertising in the Ukraine. Twenty-five billboards were counted by one observer in the distance between the airport and a city centre. (11) The prosperous, free image of "being American" permeates tobacco advertising in newly emerging eastern European countries. In Russia the first advertisement in Red Square promoted a brand of cigarette called West. In Poland, the words *really American* are synonymous with L & M brands. (12)

Governments of China, India, Vietnam, Korea and former Warsaw pact countries receive a major source of income from cigarette taxes. (13) Bribed politicians are persuaded to turn a blind eye as tobacco promotes its deadly products with the impunity it once enjoyed in the western world.

Tobacco Advertising Budget – 1997
(F.T.C. Report To Congress pursuant to the Federal Cigarette Labeling & Advertising Act (issued July 28, 1999)

Unfortunates in third world countries suffer and starve due to lack of funding for food and medical resources. The tobacco cartel's priorities begin and end with promoting their product.

Promotional allowances, including payments to retailers for shelf space $ 2.44 billion

Discount coupons, sales promos ('buy one/get one free'), gift bonuses $1.52 billion

Branded specialty items promotional events other than point-of-sale $ 512.6 million

Cigarette samples to the public $22.1 million

Newspaper advertising $17 million

Magazine advertising $237 million

Outdoor advertising $295.3 million

Point-of-sale advertising $305.4 million

Internet advertising (geared to attract underage buyers of tobacco) $215,000

In 1997, no money or other compensation was reported to have been paid to facilitate cigarette brand names or tobacco products' appearance in any motion picture or television shows. This deception through silence belies the muzzled co-operation between tobacco companies, studios and actors involving payment for surreptitious display of cigarette logos in movies, to guarantee smoking would be portrayed as the social norm by Hollywood-produced entertainment perceived by the public to represent reality. Ten years ago, smoking was portrayed in movies on average of every twenty minutes. That has now been stepped up and moviegoers will see someone on the screen in some smoking-related activity on average of every three minutes. On May 12, 1998, ASH Action for Smoking and Health announced at a press conference its filing of a formal complaint with the U.S. Department of Justice over product placement by cigarette manufacturers. ASH was joined by the American Lung Association, the American Medical Women's Association, Congressman James V. Hansen, Congressman William Luther, the National Medical Association, the Public Citizen and U.S. PIRG. "Product placement" describes industry paying to have their brands appear in movies for compensation. (14)

Philip Morris "didn't pay his bills out of the goodness of their heart," "That was a means of buying his silence and his cooperation so he would not be a spokesman for the opposite position." Stanley Rosenblatt commenting on Philip Morris paying $10 million a year of legal expenses for Liggett Group Tobacco Company's owner Bennett LeBow, who implied he would go public with the information they all knew. In March 1996 Bennett LeBow was the first tobacco executive to acknowledge publicly that cigarettes are addictive and cause cancer. *Detroit News: Tobacco Giant Philip Morris is Accused of Buying Silence.* **July 22, 1997.**

"Fuomo Loco" Tobacco Alive and Well in Brazil

Tobacco's own research scientists can be considered the world-class experts on the addictiveness of nicotine and the consequences of smoking. They have known since the 1950's the potency of nicotine and the extent of devastation to health caused by smoking. In 1961 Sir Charles Ellis, British American Tobacco's Director of Research wrote to his colleagues describing smokers as "nicotine addicts". (15)

Laboratory rats confirmed two indicators of addiction when they self-administered nicotine by pressing levers to inject themselves with regulated doses, and over time developed a tolerance for nicotine – that means the same dose eventually produced a diminished effect. Nicotine research was conducted in heavily secured, top-secret laboratories owned by Philip Morris in Germany, and by Brown & Williamson in Geneva, Switzerland and Harrogate, England. In a 1977 memorandum from Philip Morris research scientist William Dunn, the comment was made that should their research confirm that nicotine is addictive, "We will bury it". (16)

Voluntary disclosure of negative news has not been tobacco's usual style. In 1963, Brown & Williamson rejected corporate counsel's advice to disclose to the U.S. Surgeon General the results of tobacco research about the addictive quality of nicotine. More than thirty years of silent deception would pass before nicotine's addictiveness could no longer be denied. Thirty years equates to many billions in profits – and a general public who believed if cigarettes were so harmful, surely someone would say so?

From 1955 to 1980, levels of nicotine in American-grown tobacco increased by 50% as the result of industry genetic engineering of tobacco plants. Brown & Williamson covertly cultivated the Y-1 tobacco plant which contained double the nicotine content of tobacco previously grown. Developed in U.S. laboratories, the seeds for this strain of tobacco plant were smuggled by a Brown & Williamson executive into Brazil, in direct contravention of U.S. export law. (17)

Grown in Brazil in the high country of Rio Grande de Sol, Y-1 is so potent it must be diluted with weaker tobaccos to avoid smokers becoming sick from nicotine overdose. Growers sell their tobacco crops to Souza Cruz, a Brazilian company owned by the American Brown & Williamson Tobacco.

Y-1 tobacco, packing twice the nicotine punch of regularly grown U.S. tobacco crops, was shipped to the U.S. and used in five of Brown & Williamson's cigarette brands, including three which claimed to be "light". (18) Brown & Williamson denied to the FDA investigators the company had any involvement in "any breeding of tobacco for high or low nicotine levels". (19) On further investigation, the FDA discovered two United States Customs Service invoices showing more than 250 tons of Y-1 tobacco had been shipped from Souza Cruz in Brazil to Brown & Williamson in the U.S. Brown & Williamson not only could no longer deny they had developed and grown tobacco with genetically increased nicotine levels, but were forced to disclose their American store of Y-1 tobacco in the U.S. totalled close to four million pounds. (20)

The Y-1 tobacco, developed the nickname *Fuomo Loco* (crazy tobacco) by the Brazilian growers not just for the speed at which it grows, but for the double strength nicotine hit it offers . Brown & Williamson denied genetic engineering for any reason other than to develop a tobacco producing a lower rate of tar content.

The public statements of tobacco executives differ so greatly from their internal memos, at first glance you could be forgiven for thinking the comments refer to something other than tobacco. The deception through keeping silent about promoting a product deliberately engineered to create drug dependency has been the most damaging in tobacco's quest for respectability. Without compromising corporate secrets, they could have disclosed the information they've had for decades and issued clear warnings about the use of their products. Since nobody insisted, they said nothing.

"A time to rend, and a time to sew; a time to keep silence, and a time to speak;"Ecclesiastes 3:7

****

"There were things that I felt needed to be said" Dr. Jeffrey Wigand, "The Insider" and former Vice President of Research and Development, Brown & Williamson Tobacco.

Summary

Recent litigation has resulted in public outrage and demand for disclosure by the tobacco industry of information about its products, deliberately kept secret for many decades. Increased restrictions on the sale and consumption of tobacco in developed countries has necessitated a shift in focus on cultivating tobacco-friendly governments in the third world.

The World Health Organization tells us tobacco killed three million people worldwide in 1990. By the year 2020, tobacco deaths will rise to 8.4 million in and 10 million by the year 2030 . (21)

T.S. Eliot talks of the roar which is the other side of silence. Tobacco bank on the silence of deception.

"Very few customers are aware of the effects of nicotine,
i.e. its addictive nature and that nicotine is a poison."
Trial Exhibit 12408 (R.J. Reynolds planning memorandum,
entitled *The Nature of the Tobacco Business
and the Crucial Role of Nicotine*, written in 1972)

• V - SECOND HAND SMOKE - FIRSTHAND POLLUTION •
Tiny Smokestacks Poison a Room

"The 52 billion cigarettes smoked each year [in Canada] deliver almost 5,000 tonnes of pollutants into the atmosphere." (Physicians for a Smoke-Free Canada *Comparison of Sidestream Smoke and Air Pollution from Industry January 1999)*

Information about Secondhand Smoke

Tobacco industry commentary prefers to label secondhand smoke as *environmental tobacco smoke* (ETS), trivializing what it is: a substance known to cause cancer in humans. Use of the word "environmental" implies indigenous and natural conditions. There is nothing natural or acceptable about the toxic waste produced as the by-product of combustion from a lighted cigarette, pipe or cigar.

Nine out of ten pediatricians said cigarette smoke is the greatest environmental contributor to the number and/or severity of diseases and conditions among their patients. (1)

Secondhand smoke is the third leading cause of preventable disease, disability and death in the U.S.; the second is alcohol use; the first is active smoking. (2)

Because the organic material in tobacco doesn't burn completely, cigarette smoke contains more than 4,700 chemical compounds, including carbon monoxide, ammonia, formaldehyde, benzene and arsenic. Of these, 43 are known to cause cancer. (3)

Tobacco smoke poses two serious problems in an enclosed indoor space. Firstly, ventilation can only limit peak concentration and cannot be increased beyond what is cost effective. Based on random samples taken during a research project in Washington, D.C. metropolitan areas, 19 micro environments (bingo halls, bowling alleys, etc.) were studied where smokers smoked. Two-thirds of these locations were out of compliance with ventilation rates much less than local codes.

As a conservative average, at least one cigarette will be constantly burning for every three smokers in a room. A condensed and very basic explanation of Einstein's *gedanken* experiment illustrates why toxic tobacco smoke can never be completely removed from any indoor room. Steady generation of tobacco smoke in a room of smokers can be compared to a bathtub filled to capacity, drain open, and a steady flow of water into the tub to maintain the equilibrium. Water drains from the bathtub at the same rate as it is being filled, and the water level in the bathtub remains constant. Slowly add a big bottle of India ink to the water in the bathtub, causing the water to darken. During this ongoing process, the color of the water will become lighter, but will never clear completely.

Substitute a room of air for the water in the bathtub of water, and substitute tobacco smoke for the India ink in this analogy, and you have a simplified illustration of the mechanics of ventilation systems. Limited control can be achieved in raising and lowering concentration of tobacco smoke in the room, depending on how much ventilation is installed – and utilized - but the tobacco smoke will never be completely eliminated.

Solutions embracing increases in ventilation, the argument typically presented by the tobacco cartel, use an unrealistic hypothetical situation where inhabitants of a room remain stationery, do not increase in number, and limit their smoking to only one cigarette burning at any given time for every three smokers.

A ventilation engineer designs the system to comply with standards in ventilation codes specifying so many cubic feet per minute, per occupant. Except in the State of California, no requirement exists in the U.S. to ensure ongoing operation of the installed system according to specifications. Canadian requirements vary and remain difficult if not impossible to monitor. Complicated and expensive research becomes necessary to determine whether ventilation systems are being utilized according to code. The moment the scientist completes such research studies, no guarantees exist such a system will continue to be used in compliance with standards. Secondly, tobacco smoke conforms to the scientific definition of a toxic and carcinogenic chemical, and appears on the national list of carcinogens posted by the U.S. National Toxicology Program, on the same list as asbestos, arsenic and mustard gas for which no safe level of exposure exists.

Hands up, how many smokers would like to volunteer to go into a room where mustard gas, arsenic and asbestos are in use, or have recently been used? Tobacco smoke is no different in its toxicity. It also leaves a residue of toxic waste containing gases and particles on the ceiling, walls, floor and in the ventilation system. It is toxic waste. Smokers "choose" to inhale Class A carcinogens directly into their lungs on average of ten times with each cigarette smoked. The majority of the population whose preference is to remain smoke-free become unwillingly exposed to these poisons unless smoke-free ordinances protect them.

Until recent years, tobacco smoke exposure had been the norm. Many 'boomers' grew up with one or more smoking parents and remained ignorant of the information known by the tobacco industry about the toxic effects of secondhand smoke on nonsmokers - information the tobacco industry carefully and deliberately kept secret from the general public for many decades, until a court order forced them to disclose their research documents. Tobacco reacted by producing lists of additional dangerous commonplace substances in a transparent attempt to normalize involuntary exposure to tobacco smoke. Their soundbytes proclaiming the dangers of exhaust fumes, barbeques and perfume in elevators do nothing to alter the inherent danger of tobacco smoke. When challenged, tobacco spokespeople solemnly ruminate over global disasters such as earthquakes, floods and nuclear accidents, suggesting the smoke-free who want protection from secondhand smoke concentrate, instead, on more pressing issues. People typically discount risks with which they are familiar, and disproportionately fear risks with which they are unfamiliar.

Tobacco vindicators' tunnel vision believes only one social issue can be addressed at a time and for them, predictably, tobacco has the lowest priority. Drunk driving, drug use by teens and domestic violence – which, combined, do not claim as many lives each year as tobacco (4) - absorb tobacco supporters' total focus, leaving no time or energy to address the health outcome of tobacco use and involuntary exposure to secondhand smoke. In comical contradiction, a prominent concern always mentioned in defense of unrestricted smoking is the "real pollution" caused by vehicle exhaust, barbeques and campfires. Their list of what-about's grows ever long, while the health consequences of passive smoking remain as serious as they've ever been.

Meanwhile, tobacco's only agenda continues to be normalization of the bizarre behavior of placing a tube of dried leaves in the mouth, and setting it on fire for the sole purpose of sucking smoke directly into the lungs on average of 200 times each day for the pack a day smoker.

"Children can leave the room if they are bothered by smoke." **Reminded that infants cannot leave, he responded,** *"When they are older, they can crawl away."* **Mike Harper, the former CEO of R.J.**

Reynolds Tobacco, answered a shareholder's question in 1996 about smoking around children. (Minnesota Smoke-Free Coalition, *In Their Own Words)*

James Repace, M.Sc. and Science Policy Analyst and Staff Scientist at the U.S. Environmental Protection Agency from 1979 – 1998, has set out in an international campaign to monitor exposure to tobacco smoke effectively. This doesn't mean going into restaurants, bars and work-places to measure smoke levels, but to measure levels of the nicotine metabolite, cotinine, in bodily fluids. Results of his research confirm the exposure of the general public to tobacco smoke exceeds general opinion. The level of air pollution can be back calculated from cotinine levels and his Hong Kong study confirmed that with only one exception, every single restaurant waiter in that study violated the U.S. Environ-mental Protection Agency standards of air quality, both for the annual and the twenty-four hour standards. Tobacco apologists argue cotinine levels can be affected by nicotine content in some vegetables. To detect the equivalent cotinine concentrations present in children from house-holds where two or more family members smoke, 90 kilograms (198 lbs.) of raw tomatoes would have to be eaten *every day.* (5)

Tobacco smoke is a regulated air pollutant in terms of its impact on the lungs on fine particle concentrations in the air, and it violates all EPA standards.

Clean air never exists in any room where people are smoking. Sec-ondhand smoke contains higher concentrations of poisons than those inhaled by smokers through a filter tip. Secondhand smoke means first-hand pollution.

Secondhand Smoke Exposure is a Type of Child Abuse

James Gabarino, Director of Cornell University's Family Life Devel-opment Centre, says "More young children are killed by parental smok-ing than by all unintentional injuries combined. Let's call it what it is: Parental smoking is child abuse." (6)

Pregnant women who smoke and nonsmoking pregnant women ex-posed daily to tobacco smoke are more likely to have low birth weight babies at risk for death and disease in infancy and early childhood. (7)

Nursing mothers who smoke can pass along harmful chemicals from cigarettes to their babies in breast milk. (8)

More than one-third (35 percent) of all deaths from Sudden Infant Death Syndrome (SIDS) are due to maternal tobacco use. U.S. Children are three times more likely to die from SIDS caused by maternal smoking than die from homicide or child abuse. (9)

Children of parents who smoke have a higher prevalence of symptoms of respiratory irritation such as cough, phlegm, and wheeze. (10)

Exposure to secondhand smoke substantially increases the risk of lower respiratory tract infections, and is responsible for an estimated 350,000 cases of bronchitis and 152,000 cases of pneumonia annually or 16 percent of all lung infections in U.S. children under the age of five. (11)

Involuntary exposure to tobacco smoke is responsible for an estimated 1.2 million ear infections each year in the United States, or approximately 7 percent of the total. (12)

Children exposed to household smoking are at greater risk of requiring surgery for recurrent ear infections or tonsillitis; an estimated 86,000 tube insertions (14 percent of the total) and 18,000 tonsillectomies/adenoidectomies (removal of the tonsils or adenoids — 20 percent of the total) each year in the United States are attributable to secondhand smoke. (13)

Secondhand smoke exposure is associated with higher risk of developing asthma and more frequent and severe asthma attacks in children who already have the disease. Each year in the United States, an estimated 11 percent of all asthma cases and more than half a million physician visits for asthma are due to smoking in the home. (14)

Exposure to the smoking of one or both parents has also been shown to be a highly important predictor of smoking among adolescents. (15)

It takes more than three hours to remove 95 percent of the smoke from one cigarette from the room once smoking has ended. (16)

Secondhand Smoke and Custody Decisions

In divorce agreements, the corollary to a smoking parent who remains deluded about the harm caused by exposure to secondhand smoke is court ordered visitation restriction and in extreme cases, denial of parental rights.

In an alarming number of cases, parents place the gratification of their addiction to nicotine above not only the welfare of their child, but also jeopardize their custody rights. Court orders have been required before some smoking parents stop exposing their children to secondhand smoke. Some custody decisions influenced by parental exposure to secondhand smoke: (17)

1988, Roofeh v. Roofeh, (NY Family Ct., Nassau County, Mineola). Mr. Jahanshah Roofeh's attorney, Stephen W. Schlissel of Mineola, NY's Ruskin, Schlissel, Moscou, Evans & Faltischek, P.C.; Ms. Elizabeth Roofeh represented by Joel R. Brandes of Garden City, NY. Nassau County Judge Ralph Diamond in Mineola issued order forbidding Elizabeth to smoke in front of her husband and three children. Ms. Roofeh was also directed to confine her cigarette smoking to a small television room in the couple's Kings Point mansion. (18)

1988, Reeves v. Reeves, Pricilla Bullock (married name Reeves) complained about a judge's order restricting her from smoking in confined areas around her four-year-old son. Fourth Circuit Court Judge Bill Swann made the ruling and said his decision was based on the child's welfare. Swann granted a request by the ex-husband's lawyer to prohibit her from smoking around the child in a confined environment, such as the home or in an automobile. {Knoxville News-Sentinel, 6/4/88}

1989, Badeau v. Badeau, (LA). In LaPlace, LA, an appeals court upheld a lower court decision reducing a father's visitation rights because his smoking aggravated his child's bronchial problem. {WSJ, 10/18/90}

"I was overwhelmed about the amount of information there was that the rest of us didn't know...The documents I reviewed had 'secret' stamped all over them." — Dr. Richard Hurt, Director of the Mayo Clinic's Nicotine Dependence Center

1989, in Denton, MD, a judge placed a three-year-old girl with severe asthma in a foster home because her parents ignored medical advice to protect the child from their tobacco smoke. {WSJ, 10/18/90}

1990, De Beni Souza v. Kallweit (Sacramento, CA, August) Judge David Stirling ordered a woman (Anna Maria de Beni Souza) not to smoke in front of her five-year-old son; judge issued the ruling at the request of the boy's father, Manfred Kallweit, who had complained of health risks associated with inhaling secondhand smoke. (19)

1991, Robert Strathmann v. Linda Foster (20) Judge Stephanie Domitrovich ordered that there will be no smoking in the natural father's home for at least 48 hours before children are to visit. The natural father shall provide a smokefree environment for all of the children while he is exercising his partial custody with them. Natural mother shall also provide a smokefree environment.

1991, Mitchell v. Mitchell In this divorce case, the court refused to return custody of an asthmatic child to the mother although the mother had joined a smoking cessation program. The father had been awarded custody because the child suffered from asthma and, despite the pediatrician's advice, the mother and grandmother had not stopped smoking. The trial judge had found that the failure of the mother and grandmother to stop smoking was strong evidence of lack of proper concern for the welfare of the child. (21)

1991, Brett Lee Bryant/Department of Social Services v. Wakely, et al. The Michigan Court of Appeals upheld the decision of a Civil Court that placement with a grandmother who smoked would not be in a child's best interest. The child had serious respiratory problems and it was highly recommended that he live in close proximity to a hospital in Traverse City (where his grandparents were unable to relocate) and that he should live in a smokefree environment. (22)

1991, Lamacchia v. Lamacchia Temporary order that neither parent will smoke in front of their three-year-old son who suffers from lung ailments. (23)

1992, Sulva v. Isaacson (IL) Judge William Ward signed an order barring Isaacson from smoking when he visited his son. It was the first time in Illinois history that such an order has been signed. Alex, the son, suffers from bronchitis and it was alleged that his father's smoking might aggravate his condition. The order meant that to have a smoke this father by court order, will either have to abstain or leave his apartment every other weekend from about 9:30 a.m. Saturday to 6:30 p.m. Sunday, as well as for about a month during the summer when he has his son for visitation. One smoke in front of his son could lead to a contempt of court finding and a jail sentence of up to 6 months. (24)

1993, Masone v. Tanner A county judge granted a nonsmoking father's request to remove an 8-year-old girl from the custody of her mother, his ex-wife. The child had only 43 percent of her breathing capacity because the mother continued to violate an earlier court order, obtained five years ago, that she not smoke around or near the child. The smoking continued until the child had an asthma attack and a doctor stated that she would end-up in an emergency room if her exposure to tobacco smoke continued. The child was placed in the custody of her grandmother. (25)

1993, Montufar v. Navot Judge Orlando granted post-judgment relief to a nonsmoking father whose child, aged ten, was exposed to tobacco smoke by his mother and maternal relatives and suffered adverse effects. (26) The order stated that the custodial mother shall provide the child a complete smokefree environment in the home in which he resides. There must be no smoking by other residents or by visitors. All smoking must be carried on outdoors. The custodial mother is also under obligation to take all reasonable steps in assuring that the child is not unduly exposed to secondhand smoke. The custodial mother must remove the child from any situation or location where he is exposed to passive smoke. As far as the grandparents are concerned (they live close to the mother) the order compels the mother to remove the child from the grandparents' presence if they are smoking. There is to be no smoking in any vehicle in which the child is a passenger. (27)

National Toxicology Program Classification of Tobacco Smoke and Secondhand Smoke

In May 2000, the U.S. National Toxicology included Environmental Tobacco Smoke, Smoking and Smokeless Tobacco on its list in its biennial *Report on Carcinogens* ("RoC"). (28) This report outlines individual substances, mixtures of chemicals, or exposure circumstances which are known to be human carcinogens or which may reasonably be anticipated to be human carcinogens; it also contains information received from other federal agencies relating to estimated exposures and exposure standards or guidelines.

The National Toxicology Program Report on Carcinogens (*RoC)* classified secondhand smoke, smoking and smokeless tobacco in the same category as benzene, mustard gas, asbestos and arsenic.

Environmental tobacco smoke - Environmental tobacco smoke, generated from sidestream and exhaled mainstream smoke of cigarettes, pipes, and cigars is listed as a known human carcinogen. The *RoC* indicates this listing is based on the observed causal relationship between passive exposure to tobacco smoke and human lung cancer. The listing states that there are conclusive published studies that indicate increased risk of lung cancer in nonsmoking women living with smoking husbands or working with smoking co-workers.

Tobacco smoking - Tobacco smoking (i.e. directly inhaled tobacco smoke) is listed as a known human carcinogen. Cigarette smoking has been known to cause cancer in humans for many years, and is now considered to be the leading preventable cause of cancer in developed countries. Separate chemicals identified in tobacco smoke were already listed as carcinogens in the *RoC*. The new listing of tobacco smoking is the result of the 1996 revision in the review process that allows for the review and listing of exposure circumstances in the *RoC*.

Predictably, tobacco front groups claim secondhand smoke, smoking and smokeless tobacco also appear on the same list as "sunshine", once again illustrating their lack of understanding between "sunshine" and carcinogenic solar UV radiation and exposure to sunlamps and sunbeds. If only a parallel to sunblock cream existed to block out the harmful effects of secondhand smoke!

"What the smoker does to himself may be his business, but what the smoker does to the non-smoker is quite a different matter....six out of ten believe that smoking is hazardous to the nonsmoker's health, up sharply over the last four years... This we see as the most dangerous development yet to the viability of the tobacco industry that has yet occurred ... The issue, as we see it, is no longer what the smoker does to himself, but what he does to others." "[Philip Morris' world-wide strategy is to] coordinate and pay so many scientists on an international basis to keep the environmental tobacco smoke controversy alive." (Roper Organization. A Study of Public Attitudes toward Cigarette Smoking and the Tobacco Industry in 1978. Vol. 1. Roper Organization, 1978)

Smoke-free Workplace Safety

Riddle: How many employers insist their staff must involuntarily be exposed to dangerous limits of heavy metals, Class A Carcinogens and poisons not allowed to be dumped in sanitary landfill sites?
Answer: All those employers who receive funding from the tobacco industry to resist clean indoor air ordinances.

In addition to the toxicity of individual chemicals contained in tobacco smoke, the chemicals contained in tobacco smoke interact with each other, enhancing and increasing toxicity and carcinogenicity. Many of the poisons contained in secondhand smoke do not need to be inhaled to cause harm. They are absorbed through the skin, and include the following: (29)

Chemicals in Secondhand Smoke (absorbed through skin contact) Carcinogenic to Humans:

4-Aminobiphenyl has been called one of the most potent known bladder carcinogens and absorption occurs through the skin.

Benzene is known to cause leukemia in humans, produce chromosomal aberrations and can take 2 – 50 years to manifest following exposure. Benzene exposure occurs in absorption through the skin.

2-Aminonaphthalene causes cancer in humans and is absorbed both by inhalation and through the skin.

Vinyl Chloride causes lung and liver cancer in humans. It is readily absorbed through the skin.

Cadmium, Nickel and Polonium-210 (Radon) are also present in secondhand smoke. Exposure to these chemicals through inhalation causes cancer in humans.

Chemicals in Secondhand Smoke (absorbed through the skin) Possibly and Probably Carcinogenic to Humans

1-Aminonaphthalene used industrially for dyes and weed control, has been shown to cause lung, liver and leukemia cancers in animals. Absorption through the skin can occur without any irritation or other warning.

Acetaldehyde Animal studies in which pregnant rats were exposed found that acetaldehyde gave birth to offspring with growth retardation, malformation, delayed bone growth and stillbirth. Small amounts of acetaldehyde irritates the eyes, skin and respiratory tract of humans and animals.

Acetone is a irritant to eyes, nose and throat and causes liver damage. Absorption occurs through inhalation and skin contact.

Acrylonitrile is suspected to cause cancer in humans, and is similar to cyanide in toxicity. Acrylonitrile is also known as vinyl cyanide. Pregnant animals exposed to acrylonitrile showed significant maternal toxicity and increase in deformed fetuses and offspring. It is absorbed from the respiratory and gastrointestinal tract and through skin contact.

Benzo[a]pyrene has been found to cause cancer in animals and fish in every study to date. Absorption occurs through inhalation and through skin contact. When combined with catechol (also in tobacco smoke), the result is co-carcinogenic.

Cresol promotes tumors in mice, and long term human exposure results in headaches, nausea, vomiting and impaired kidney function.

It is absorbed through the skin.

Lead is known to cause cancer in animals, and is soluble in body fluids when inhaled. Lead poisoning effects on the brain may not be reversible, and long term exposure may lead to kidney disease.

Phenol damages the lungs and central nervous system, irritates the skin, mucous membranes and eyes of humans. It is absorbed by inhalation and through the skin.

Quinoline causes genetic mutations and prolonged exposure causes liver damage and nosebleeds. Absorption occurs by inhalation and through the skin.

"Carcinogens are found in practically every class of compounds in smoke...flavor substances and carcinogenic substances come from the same classes, in many instances." Confidential Philip Morris report *Tobacco and Health Research & Development Approach page seventeen November 15, 1961   Bates number 2024947191*

The battle for improved standards of occupational health and safety has been long and hard and is far from over. California leads the way for strict smoke-free legislation, designating outdoor or separately enclosed smoking areas for the one in four of the general population who is addicted to nicotine and cannot make it through a working day without nicotine fixes at regular intervals.

British Columbia, Canada has fought the tobacco front groups who claim smoke-free bars and restaurants harm the hospitality industry. In British Columbia, self-appointed and tobacco-funded front groups with names like Barwatch and Coalition of Hospitality Organizations come and go as the Pacific tides. They represent less than 5% of the hospitality industry in that province, whose official union, CAW, supports improved workplace safety for their members, guaranteed by smoke-free legislation.

In 1999 the tobacco industry made available $800,000 for their Courtesy of Choice campaign in Canada to fund their front groups who launch frivolous lawsuits and make headlines with pseudo-sob stories about businesses gone belly-up because the one in five members of the population in British Columbia who smoke can no longer do so beyond the boundaries of outdoor patios and designated smoking areas. In Vancouver, those establishments who claimed their business suffered during a six-week smoking ban in January, 2000 were the same places who did not comply with the smoke-free ordinance. (30)

The Ventilation Non-Solution

Predictably, the tobacco industry retaliates against efforts to protect the smoke-free from secondhand smoke by diverting the focus away from the known health risks of tobacco smoke exposure towards the fabricated notion that ordinances and occupational health and safety standards infringe on the "rights of business" to "decide for themselves". Their strategy leaves nothing to chance:

"1.   Mobilize all scientific studies of indoor air quality (e.g., radon, wood stoves, gas stoves, formaldehyde, asbestos, etc.) into a general indictment of the air we breathe indoors. Use a scientific front - especially some liberal Nader group.

2.   Use this material to fuel PR offensive on poor indoor air quality.

3.   Create a model indoor air quality bill to be added to suggested state legislation book published annually. Model bill will focus on ventilation, filters, inspections, etc. Smoking will not [sic] be dealt with directly.

4.   Make presentations to all trade associations (USC of C, NMA, API, etc.) on the real [sic] indoor air quality issue.

5.   Organize firms like ACVA into a travelling road show to hawk their wares to government and businesses, much like the antis sell their advice to business and government on smoking policies.

To execute this program would require money, staff time and a first-rate PR firm." (31)

The government of California did not allow this strategy to succeed. The government of British Columbia hesitated before standing up to tobacco scientists. One by one, municipal and county and provincial/state governments in Canada and the U.S. have decided not to allow big tobacco to decide standards of occupational health and safety for workers under their jurisdiction. Business has improved. Employee health has improved. The tables are slowly turning, and the only suffering we see is tobacco industry sales every time a smoker cannot smoke at work.

Smokers Deemed 'Disabled' in B.C.

The tobacco industry fosters the perception of smoking restrictions being a violation of civil liberties, and they advocate loudly that businesses have the "right to choose" what happens on their own premises.

This clearly only applies when the choice involves smoking.

In Trail, B.C., Cominco , a large smelting and iron company, enacted a smoking policy in 1998 prohibiting smoking anywhere on the company's 182 hectare property. This smoking ban included parking lots and employees' cars parked on company property, and extended the existing ban encompassing work areas with high risk of explosion from dust concentration. Cominco claimed lead and zinc increased smoking workers' health risks, and referred to dangers of secondhand smoke and potential transmission of contaminants from the smelter to employees who smoke without properly washing their hands. Cominco offered free enrolment in smoking-cessation programs weeks prior to the enactment of the extended smoke-free workplace rule.

Predictably, the 500 smoking employees protested. Cominco employs 1,900 at their Trail plant and office. An arbitrator upheld Cominco's policy as legal; however in his 138 page decision he expressed concern about the consequences of noncompliance resulting in termination of employment. Consequently, nicotine addiction was declared to be a disability, and therefore not subject to discrimination. (32) Cominco was directed, against their expressed wishes, to provide designated smoking areas in their own buildings, on their own property, to accommodate smokers who could not make it through a working shift without nicotine.

At a dollar a pack, even the lightest of workplace smoking restrictions is costing this industry $233 million a year in revenue. How much more will it cost us with far more restrictive laws ...?" 1985 Tobacco Institute Speech: *Public Smoking – The Problem* **TIMN 0014565**

Summary

The smoke emitted from the end of a lighted nicotine delivery device complies with all industrial standards to define toxic waste. Each cigarette emulates a tiny smokestack in the type of pollution it creates. The tobacco cartel prefer the term *environmental tobacco smoke* in an attempt to imply the environment naturally includes tobacco smoke.

Due to small lungs and overall size, children suffer greatly from exposure to tobacco smoke. During pregnancy, smoking mothers place at avoidable risk a healthy gestation and safe delivery of their babies. Courts of law have imposed non-smoking restrictions on those chil-

dren whose parents and grandparents place satisfaction of their nicotine addiction above the welfare of children in their care. In divorce
settlements, custody battles have been lost by smoking parents who
cared more for cigarettes than prime custody of their children .

Tobacco provides sufficient funding for front groups to oppose improved standards of workplace safety that include protection of the
majority of workers from the secondhand tobacco smoke of the minority who are addicted to nicotine. Tobacco apologists typically gloss
over any concern about daily exposure to cigarette smoke, diverting
the focus to other social concerns and long range risks of global
nuclear contamination.

Tobacco's claim that private businesses should be "free to choose"
does not apply to those businesses who choose smoke-free.

Tobacco promotes its product to prevail over the free choice of anyone who rejects it.

"Let's just say they take their
'no smoking' policy very seriously."

by kind permission of The QuitSmoking Co.

• VI - TOBACCO AND THE P.R. WAR •
Two Sides of the Same Tarnished Coin

"I've learned from experience that as soon as I'm identified as a representative of the Tobacco Institute, I lose all credibility. They just sneer us away... so I try to work behind the scenes whenever I can." *(Rob Saldana, Tobacco Institute. Los Angeles Times August 24, 1986)*

Conjuring a positive public image for Big Tobacco grows increasingly difficult. Irrefutable evidence of the decades of deceit and greed, now a matter of public record, dilute whatever efforts tobacco companies make to appear as responsible members of any community. The tobacco industry struggles to justify sales of a product which, when used as directed, creates addiction, disease, suffering and premature death. Tobacco PR attempts include organizing phony grassroots groups that lobby for the tobacco industry, and create biased "video news releases" that air during carefully scheduled news hours, attempting to imply their carefully orchestrated paid advertising is authentic TV journalism, news flashes or a mini-documentary.

The tobacco cartel could address World Health Organization allegations that its product kills three million people each year, worldwide. Instead, Philip Morris spends $2.3 million on thirty second television advertisements declaring solemn concern for the disadvantaged who happen to be among the same members of society defined in their Project S.C.U.M. (also called Health and Morality Counter Campaign), describing how they have stepped up exports abroad to "compensate for the shrinking domestic market". (1) For every dollar spent to "make a difference", Philip Morris spends $1.30 on prime time advertising space to publicize their unique brand of philanthropy, which is supported by an industry that kills its most loyal customers by the hundreds of thousands every year in the U.S. alone. (2)

On Philip Morris' website, they proudly proclaim their first disaster relief donation was made to the Red Cross in 1960 to aid earthquake victims in Chile. An interesting choice of philanthropy in a severely troubled world – but not surprising when Chilean tobacco interests are taken into account. Tobacco farming contributes to Chile's economy, and in 1979 International Tobacco Marketing S.A. (Chile) became a Philip Morris affiliate.

Tobacco traditionally provides funding for those projects guaranteed to catch the attention of politicians who can be useful when smoke-free proposals arrive at the stage of implementation. In the province of British Columbia, Canada, a month following his election victory as Premier, Gordon Campbell admitted to receiving $5,000 from a to-bacco front group. Apparently he sees no conflict of interest in receiv-ing tobacco election campaign money and his government's nullifica-tion of the 100% smoke-free workplace legislation due to be imple-mented two months following his election to office. (3)

Shortly after election in the U.S., President George W. Bush rein-stated tobacco's previously prohibited facility to advertise tobacco prod-ucts on billboards near schools and playgrounds. Karl Rove, one of Bush's campaign strategists and chief political advisor since the 1980's was paid by tobacco from 1991 – 1996 as a "paid political intelligence operative". For obtaining information on federal, state and local-level political activities, Rove admitted to receiving a retainer from Philip Morris of up to $3,000 per month. (4) Two more close friends and advisors, well known for their tobacco lobbying in Washington, in-clude James Francis Jr. and Haley Barbour. (5) Bush supports tort reform limiting consumers' rights to sue corporations, and opposes in-creasing taxes on tobacco. Tobacco strategy traditionally includes buy-ing support from policymakers. Tobacco tentacles reach far and to-bacco eyes and ears miss nothing.

Tobacco philanthropy has its best illustration with the multi-mil-lion dollar advertising campaign Philip Morris proclaim as their ef-forts to make a difference. 4-H (Head, Heart, Hands, Health) a well respected youth organization, accepted financing from Philip Morris. In exchange, Philip Morris has representation on the 4-H Program Design Committee for the 4-H tobacco prevention campaign. Philip Morris know better than anyone how 90% of smokers begin by the age of 18. Tobacco documents outline the importance of recruiting "replace-ment smokers", found in the 14 – 17 year old age bracket.

In the U.S., charitable donations to non-profit groups bring a tax deduction. While this does not go un-noticed in Philip Morris' *making a difference* scam, their main mandate has been to raise their public profile as a responsible and caring member of the community. In these efforts, they make no mention whatsoever of the six year olds who smoke ciga-rettes in India and the distribution of free cigarettes to youth in those countries whose governments look the other way for a good tobacco bribe. The only difference the tobacco cartel apparently wants to make is to increase profits and return social acceptance of its products to the status they enjoyed half a century ago. Any industry who truly wanted to make a difference would not focus its efforts on manufacturing and marketing what their scientists call drug delivery devices, carefully engineered to addict new customers at a target rate of 3,000 every day.

Any industry who has genuine concern about children, would not consider the heart and health aspects of the 4H programme as profit fodder. (6)

"...Expand involvement of Corporate in making grants to public policy organizations and continue identifying grants that are special interest to key elected officials. Also take advantage of Disaster Relief Budget to involve governors in check presentations." *Public Affairs Budget Presentation* **September 28, 1993 Bates Number 2044712624/2687**

Tobacco front groups abound and typically arrive in three distinct packages. The first calls itself many variations of a "smokers' rights" group of indignant and outraged citizens , some of whom will claim to be non-smokers, but "concerned about government interference". These groups unite to protest what they claim to be threats against individual freedoms caused by smoking restrictions prohibiting smokers from exposing the smoke-free to involuntary passive smoking. The most illustrious group of this type has been the National Smokers Alliance, fronted by $4 million seed money from Philip Morris, BATCO and Lorillard. A polished and professional public relations firm, Burson Marstellar handles tobacco P.R. and prides itself on its ability to create grassroots organizations, also known as astroturf tobacco lobbying.

These front groups of "concerned citizens" can be assembled in hours from tobacco's database of smokers and sympathizers. When Philip Morris withdrew its support from the National Smokers Alliance in 1998, the Centre for Individual Freedoms appeared at the same address, and Walker Merryman of the Tobacco Institute said "All we're going to do is change the name on the door. We're going to continue to do what we've always done."(7)

Burson Marstellar, one of the largest public relations firms in the world, works hard for its Philip Morris tobacco dollars. An important aspect of credibility involves careful and deliberate selection of labels for tobacco front groups. The Californians for Statewide Smoking Restrictions promoted Prop 188, the 1994 ballot intended to weaken existing smoking bans. "Restaurants for Sensible Voluntary Policy" and "California Business and Restaurant Alliance" protested smoke-free workplace legislation for the hospitality industry in California. California leads the way to smoke-free workplace legislation and their experience illustrates sly tobacco tactics used everywhere. In areas where smoke-free workplace legislation is proposed, restaurant owners receive unsolicited visits from paid tobacco employees who present "research" to indicate business suffers drastically following smoking bans. They advise restaurant owners of scheduled city council meetings, provide transportation to attend, and accompany them. Individuals who have been identified as tobacco employees appear on a list of forty tobacco industry front groups known to the Americans for Nonsmokers Rights. Once their cover is blown, front groups simply change their name and carry on.

Tobacco public relations experts never allow the truth to get in their way. Gwyn Bicker of Burson-Marstellar's Sacramento office was presented with sales and tax returns confirming business does not suffer following smoking bans – and in many cases, improves. She replied by asking whether the figures presented are because of the smoking ban, or the "general turnaround of the economy". When told the same questions apply to her own information on alleged business losses due to smoking bans, she dismissively answered by saying, "It's a hit-and-miss issue. It's hard to get your arms around it." (8)

People United for Friendly Smoking, American Smokers Alliance, American Tort Reform Association, California Citizens for Common Sense, Restaurants for a Sensible Voluntary Policy: where smoking restrictions are enacted or proposed, you can guarantee any organization protesting them who calls itself *concerned* and *sensible* has only one agenda: to promote the interests of tobacco and stem the tide of smoke-free workplaces.

The second type of tobacco front group appears as "independent scientific research". One such organization, the Oakridge National Laboratory (ORNL) has received over $1 million from the Council for Tobacco Research and the Centre for Indoor Air Research. (9) Scientists working for these tobacco funded "independent" research organizations are typically proffered as expert witnesses in tobacco trials. Their tobacco-bankrolled "research" attempts to defend the consequences of unwilling workplace exposure to the Class A carcinogens, heavy metals and poisons in secondhand smoke, and exonerate the tobacco industry from any responsibility for illness caused by it. Additional tobacco fronted "scientific research" organizations include International Technology

Corporation of Tennessee, Government Consultants International – who did not disguise their tobacco connection very well in the title of their report R.J.R. MacDonald Environmental Tobacco Smoke Survey. (10)

Chapter III *Tobacco Brand of Science* details more pseudo-scientific efforts to divert attention from conclusive evidence about the harm caused to everyone who comes into contact with tobacco smoke.

"Nicotine is the addicting agent in cigarettes." Memorandum from A.J. Mellman to R.A. Blott, B & W Project Recommendations (March 25, 1983). Trial Exhibit #13344

The Association of American Physicians and Surgeons (AAPS) formally state "We don't think people should smoke but it should not be used as an excuse for government intrusion into private decisions." (11) Compare their statement with the clear condemnation of tobacco from the American Academy of Pediatrics (AAP - no "s") Policy Statement on tobacco: "A tobacco-free environment is imperative, because tobacco is a major health hazard to infants, children, adolescents, and their families. Parental use of tobacco has significant adverse effects on pregnancy and fetal outcome". (12)

The AAP (no "s") was founded in 1930 and is a not-for-profit corporation organized for scientific and educational purposes with a membership of 55,000 pediatricians, pediatric sub-specialists and pediatric surgical specialists in the United States, Canada and Latin America , 34,000 of whom are board certified.(13)

The AAPS was founded in 1943 and release no information about their sources of funding.

The third type of tobacco front group recruits local businesses to form coalitions against proposed smoking restrictions. Once again, the focus is deliberately and carefully shifted away from public health concerns of involuntary exposure to tobacco smoke, and directed towards the ferociously protected domain of civil rights. The emphasis always rests exclusively with the rights and choices of smokers. The rights and choices of the majority of the population who are not tobacco consumers, without exception, do not warrant a mention. Anyone who requests respect for a smoke-free choice is typically portrayed as controlling and unreasonable.

In their strategy paper, the conclusion is clear: "The hospitality industry is our greatest ally" and the mandate , without question: "to enlist participants in order to strengthen our support" : *Philip Morris and the Hospitality Industry: Our Mission: To maintain the Ability for Our Consumers to Enjoy Our Products in Public Venues.* Three arenas are identified for "fighting" legislation for clean indoor air. In the 17 Class A states: "protect existing preemption". In 8 Class B states: "pass statewide accommodation/preemption" and Class C states: "prevent pending bans; overturn existing bans". Those remaining states classified as Class C receive the most attention in the clear plan stating "All resources, contacts, relationships, research, database, etc. will be activated in an all-out fight." (14)

Sample names of tobacco fronted hospitality coalitions in Canada include: Association for the Respect of Smokers' Rights; Smokers' Freedom Society (received $100,000 from tobacco) (15);Hospitality Coalition; Lower Mainland Hospitality Industry Group; Coalition of Hospitality Organizations; Barwatch; PUBCO in Ontario (who refuse to release a list of their members and benefactors); B.C. Liquor Licensee and Retailers Association. The Benson & Hedges 'Business Edge' program has a simple strategy: bribing pub owners to install cigarette vending machines, referred to in typical tobacco euphemism as "exclusive distribution channels".

In addition to the National Smokers Alliance and the Centre for Individual Freedom, U.S. tobacco front groups include the Empire State Restaurant and Tavern Association (who also used the aliases the New York Tavern and Restaurant Association, the Manhattan Tavern and Restaurant Association and the United Restaurant, Hotel and Tavern Association). In 1995, this organization received $553,204 through its Empire State Restaurant and Tavern Association moniker to enable it to fight clean indoor air proposals in Albany, New York. When pressed for receipts, the Tobacco Institute later disclosed they had under-reported their support to this organization by $443,072. (16)

Other names of tobacco funded organizations and front groups have included Valley Business Owners and Concerned Citizens, Oregon Restaurant Association, Contributions Watch (CW), State Affairs Company (SAC), APCO & Associates. Contributions Watch calls itself a "public interest" and "reform" organization of "concerned citizens". Its mandate has always been very focused: attack the messenger who brings the unwelcome-to-tobacco messages and do whatever it takes to shift attention away from the negative health consequences of smoking.

All tobacco front advocacy groups collectively face a dilemma described in one commentary, "How do you pose as an idealistic crusader for full disclosure while simultaneously hiding your special-interest agenda?" The answer, as usual, rests with expert legal advice. (17)

Philip Morris rewarded CW's deep concern for consumer issues by paying the organization $65,547.86 for "services rendered" from August 1, 1996 to August 31, 1996. (18) Promotion of tobacco interests disguises itself as "accommodation" programs such as the Red Light – Green Light fiasco. When California was in the process of enacting 100% smoke-free workplaces, tobacco attempted to "confound the antis" with a "flurry of legislative activity". They filed lawsuits challenging the government's right to implement smoking bans. They state their intention to file a ballot initiative seeking a state preemption bill to "accommodate" smokers. (19) California has been smoke-free since January 1, 1998. Subsequent research confirms smoking bans result in improved health for hospitality staff and no adverse affects for business. (20)

"Smoking restrictions have been estimated this year alone to have decreased PM profits by $40 million" *Public Affairs Budget Presentation* **September 28, 1993 Bates Number 2044712624/2687**

The Tobacco Institute

A prime illustration for every aspect of the negative and self-serving agenda of a powerful public relations machine exists in the Tobacco Institute, an unparalleled example of carefully orchestrated and expensive publicity used to work against public health and occupational safety. The Tobacco Institute, funded by the endless reserve of tobacco resources, spared no expense to undermine health professionals and consumer policy advocates.

The earliest significant effort of the Tobacco Institute (and its Council for Tobacco Research affiliate) appeared in 1954 when the first substantive research became public, linking cigarette smoking and cancer. A full-page promotion appearing in 400 American newspapers with target readership of 43 million *A Frank Statement to Cigarette Smokers* addressed the persistent medical and scientific evidence outlining the devastating health consequences of smoking. (21)

In 1954 the tobacco industry had its own research files confirming the addictive qualities of nicotine and the negative effects of smoking. Those files remained well hidden from the public eye, while this *Frank Statement* attempted to reassure smokers about cigarettes:

"A Frank Statement to Smokers" 1954

"RECENT REPORTS on experiments with mice have given wide publicity to a theory that cigarette smoking is in some way linked with lung cancer in human beings.

Although conducted by doctors of professional standing, these experiments are not regarded as conclusive in the field of cancer research. However, we do not believe results are inconclusive, should be disregarded or lightly dismissed. At the same time, we feel it is in the public interest to call attention to the fact that eminent doctors and research scientists have publicly questioned the claimed significance of these experiments.

Distinguished authorities point out:

That medical research of recent years indicates many possible causes of lung cancer.

That there is no agreement among the authorities regarding what the cause is.

That there is no proof that cigarette smoking is one of the causes.

That statistics purporting to link cigarette smoking with the disease could apply with equal force to any one of many other aspects of modern life. Indeed the validity of the statistics themselves is questioned by numerous scientists.

We accept an interest in people's health as a basic responsibility, paramount to every other consideration in our business

We believe the products we make are not injurious to health.

We always have and always will cooperate closely with those whose task it is to safeguard the public health.

For more than 300 years tobacco has given solace, relaxation, and enjoyment to mankind. At one time or another during those years critics have held it responsible for practically every disease of the human body. One by one these charges have been abandoned for lack of evidence.

Regardless of the record of the past, the fact that cigarette smoking today should even be suspected as a cause of a serious disease is a matter of deep concern to us.

Many people have asked us what we are doing to meet the public's concern aroused by the recent reports. Here is the answer:

We are pledging aid and assistance to the research effort into all phases of tobacco use and health. This joint financial aid will of course be in addition to what is already being contributed by individual companies.

For this purpose we are establishing a joint industry group consisting initially of the undersigned. This group will be known as TOBACCO INDUSTRY RESEARCH COMMITTEE.

In charge of the research activities of the Committee will be a scientist of unimpeachable integrity and national repute. In addition there will be an Advisory Board of scientists disinterested in the cigarette industry. A group of distinguished men from medicine, science, and education will be invited to serve on this Board. These scientists will advise the Committee on its research activities.

This statement is being issued because we believe the people are entitled to know where we stand on this matter and what we intend to do about it."

The Tobacco Industry Research Committee
5400 Empire State Building New York 1, NY
Sponsors:
THE AMERICAN TOBACCO COMPANY *Paul M. Hahn, President*
BENSON & HEDGES *Joseph Cullman, Jr., President*
BRIGHT BELT WAREHOUSE ASSOCIATION *F.S. Royster, President*
BROWN & WILLIAMSON TOBACCO CORPORATION *Timothy V. Hartnett, President*
BURLEY AUCTION WAREHOUSE ASSOCIATION *Albert Clay, President*
BURLEY TOBACCO GROWERS CO-OPERATIVE *John W. Jones, President*
LARUS & BROTHER COMPANY, INC. *W.T. Reed, Jr., President*
P. LORILLARD COMPANY *Kerbert A. Kent, Chairman*
MARYLAND TOBACCO GROWERS ASSOCIATION *Samuel C. Linson, General Manager*
PHILIP MORRIS & CO. LTD., INC. *O. Parker McComas, President*
R.J. REYNOLDS TOBACCO COMPANY *E. A. Darr, President*
STEPHANO BROTHERS, INC. *C.S. Stephano, D.Sc., Director of Research*
TOBACCO ASSOCIATES, INC. (An organization of flue-cured tobacco growers) *J.B. Hudson, President*
UNITED STATES TOBACCO COMPANY *J.W. Peterson, President.*
    The lies had only just begun.

"We cannot say ETS is "safe" and if we do, this is a "dangerous" statement... If smokers get message that their smoke kills others, is this not something major? "June 24, 1987 Philip Morris legal memorandum *Operation Down Under* Bates Number 2021502102

The Tobacco Institute Research Committee changed its name in 1963 to the Council for Tobacco Research, with a staff of 120 and an annual budget of $20 million. Tobacco have never been short on funds to maintain expensive public relations campaigns promoting their product and casting doubt on scientific and medical professionals who challenge their billion dollar annual profits.

The Council for Tobacco Research funded 1,200 research projects with a total cost of $154 million. (22) Much early research did conclude that smoking does indeed create significantly increased risk for some disease. Concentration of efforts shifted away from this inconvenient information. Public statements were made claiming at a "molecular level" it could not be said with certainty what "mechanism" causes disease, and since all those studies "could be wrong", further research would be required. (23)

In 1960, the Tobacco Institute's President, George Allen, said "We must learn to distinguish between the real facts of tobacco from unjustified emotional campaigns, based on the 'health scare' — a technique that was not successful 100 or 300 years ago and, we are confident, will not be successful today." (24) The tobacco cartel remain the only ones still in any doubt about what they call the "continuing controversy" of what happens to the human body when it smokes.

"The first is concerned with the ethical question: Is it morally permissible to develop a safe method for administering a habit-forming drug when, in so doing, the number of addicts will increase?"1978 Liggett Group memorandum discussing the problems of developing a less hazardous, or "safe" cigarette. *Associated Press* February 26, 1998

"...cigarettes are marketed without health claims. They're marketed for smokers, for smoking enjoyment. That's what smokers get...So it's a matter of the difference between nicotine in different products that are sold with a health claim and cigarettes that are sold for smoking pleasure as a consumer product in the

same way that coffee with caffeine is. I mean, that's the basic difference when you have to look at the nicotine issue. " Brennan Dawson, Senior Vice President of the Tobacco Institute *Smoke Screening, Online News Hour* August 23, 1996

Some Tobacco Institute Moments

"You've heard the numbers. Our industry has faced more than 1,200 smoking restriction bills in the last 15 years, with a better than 90 per cent success rate....We have 17 professional field staff battling these proposals. They are assisted by lobbyists in each state capital and in local jurisdictions as appropriate. Our volunteer Tobacco Action Network now numbers 85,000; of these, about 12,000 have been identified as activists who can be relied upon to act when the call for help goes out. Yet, we are badly outnumbered by the voluntary health organizations who can call upon more than 3 million members or volunteers nationwide." (25)

"Those who say they work under [smoking] restrictions smoked about one-and-a-quarter fewer cigarettes each day than those who don't. That may sound light, but remember we're talking about light restrictions, too.... Those 220 people in our survey who work under smoking restrictions represent some 15 million Americans. That one-and-one-quarter per day cigarette reduction, then, means nearly 7 billion fewer cigarettes smoked each year because of workplace smoking restrictions... That's 350 million packs of cigarettes. At a dollar a pack, even the lightest of workplace smoking restrictions is costing this industry 233 million dollars a year in revenue. How much more will it cost us with far more restrictive laws such as those in Suffolk County and Fort Collings now being enacted?" (26)

"What do these health claims, the heightened public sentiment for smoking restriction, increasing nonsmoker annoyance toward smokers mean for this industry? Lower sales, of course." (27)

"Shook, Hardy [law firm] reminds us, I'm told, that the entire matter of addiction is the most potent weapon a prosecuting attorney can have in a lung cancer/cigarette case. We can't defend continued smoking as 'free choice' if the person was addicted." (28)

"More and more corporations are voluntarily banning smoking in their workplaces Consider ways THE INSTITUTE might combat them" (29)

"Might work if we could wrap smoker discrimination into a package of other credible forms of discrimination. Industry will not take this attack lightly and will fight back fiercely. We would have to have a strong attack and a good defense." (30)

Witness Project

In its persistent and unrelenting efforts to undermine increasing scientific and medical data condemning its products, the Tobacco Institute invented a new approach to guarantee court testimony in their favor: The Witness Project. Their document reveals their strategy to recruit experts who could be relied upon to testify that cigarette advertising was fair market practice designed to do no more than gain the patronage of smokers for one brand or another – although in the case of "a young person's decision to smoke", advertising played no part, and the choice to smoke fell under the jurisdiction of peer influence, parents and siblings. Testimony from well-rehearsed (and paid) "experts" could be guaranteed that women were not targets of tobacco, but "choose" to smoke a product advertised to keep pace with the transition of a woman's role in society, and that industry sponsorship of athletic and cultural events was better than "dependence on public funding." (31)

The law firm of Covington & Burling, representing tobacco's best interests, received the appointment to "develop the witnesses through this project" in order for the witnesses to "serve one or more functions". A select one or two would be permitted to testify at a congressional level; the remainder would submit essays to journalists and grant personal interviews. (32) No mention appears in this document of any steps to guarantee the truth of what would be said on behalf of the tobacco industry. The main focus remained consistent statements favorable to the industry, statements made by hand-picked and carefully trained ("developed") experts.

Secondhand smoke and all the connected health issues continued to present one of the more serious challenges to the tobacco industry and this is reflected in the effort and money spent to recruit and "develop" witnesses who would dispute conclusions of the medical community and the EPA about secondhand smoke and the harm it causes. Lawyer John Rupp of Covington & Burley outlines a memo establishing the "Asia ETS Project" . (33)

Extensive recruitment and training in the first year of this undertaking covered Malaysia, China, Singapore, Hong Kong, Indonesia, Taiwan, the Philippines and Korea. Japan Tobacco Industry co-operated with additional recruitment in Japan. Two consultants were hand-picked for their status in their home communities: Dr. Wongphanich was important to recruit because of her position as president of the Asian Association of Occupational Health; Dr. Reverente was a past president. He was due to succeed to the presidency in 1991.

Following this intensive recruitment and orientation of scientists, the Tobacco Institute publicized their gathering of 80 consulting scientists from more than twenty countries who would be presenting papers and attending a symposium hosted at McGill University.

In truth, this tobacco organized and funded "symposium" took place in space rented from McGill University, who played no part in any aspect of the gathering. (34) An additional effort at scientific credibility appeared in the thinly-disguised "Indoor Air International", a tobacco industry front group who announced plans to publish a monthly journal, inviting submissions from the participants of the "symposium." Recent recruits Drs. Bacon-Shone (Hong Kong) , Ferrer (Philippines), He (China) , Kim (Korea) , Liao (Hong Kong) , Liu (China) and Reverente (Philippines) received appointments to serve on the editorial board of "Indoor Air International" publications. Dr. Bacon-Shone proceeded to Lisbon to present a paper at a further conference (Indoor Air Quality and Ventilation in Warm Climates) consisting of a presentation geared to discredit the highly acclaimed work of Dr. Hirayama's conclusions about lung cancer among those exposed to secondhand smoke, alleging Dr. Hirayama's statistical analysis was "unsophisticated". (35)

Former Minnesota Attorney General Hubert H. "Skip" Humphrey III labelled the Tobacco Institute and the Council for Tobacco Research "twin mechanisms of past lying and conspiracy" used in tandem to fool and make fools of health officials and smokers.

January 29, 1999 both organizations closed their doors for the last time. By the time this day arrived, public relations executives following a difficult day have been heard to console themselves by saying "At least I don't work for the Tobacco Institute". (36)

"Cigarette smoking is more addictive than using heroin, hooking two-thirds of the people who ever smoke." (Dr. Robert Dupont, Director National Institute on Drug Abuse 1973-1977 TIMN 0107822)

Philip Morris Report Dead Smokers Help Economy

The most searing image of the desperation of a dinosaur industry came
to light in July, 2001 with yet another Philip Morris effort to justify
and defend tobacco, this time in a report commissioned to counter complaints from the Czechoslovakian government about the burden of health
care costs imposed by smoking-related disease and a proposed tax increase to cover them. The tobacco industry have long known increased
prices threaten sales. In a market already reeling from tobacco restrictions with smoking boomers of the 1960's succumbing to their
final tobacco-caused diseases and a public image languishing in the
gutter, Philip Morris commissioned yet another "study" to convince
the Czechoslovakian government smoking would benefit their economy.

The consulting firm of Arthur D. Little crunched the latest set of
numbers provided to them by Philip Morris to regurgitate a conclusion
that death by smoking actually aids the country's economy. The method
by which this conclusion was arrived seemed nothing more or less
than sound business to Philip Morris, whose sales pitch now includes
their allegation that since smokers die before they require old age security, medical care and housing - smoking, in truth, helps the government to balance its budget.

The report said "Our principal finding is that the negative financial
effects of smoking, such as increased health care costs, are more than
offset by positive effects (such as excise tax and VAT collected on tobacco products)... **"We calculated pension savings by multiplying the
old age pension and insurance paid from the state budget per pen-
sioner per year by the number of dead smokers of pension age in
1999...In this respect, it can also be argued that the savings are even
higher as the shortening of life means a reduction in the number of
old patients, whose treatment is more costly than average."** (37)

Percentages and subsidies and discount factors converge into this
report with little reference made to the commodity under review: human lives. Philip Morris had reached the point where their only remaining marketing ploy was to explain the financial benefits derived
by tobacco use in the of culling senior citizens.

"We assumed that in 1999, 1.7% of pensioners were in elderly housing; the annual subsidy per bed in elderly housing was 51,700CZK; 22,000
deaths were due to tobacco smoking...3.1 years of life were lost by smokers of pension age, and we applied a discount factor of 6.75%." (38)

From page seven of the report: "The negative effects of smoking on public finance take the form of increased health-care costs, the effects of early mortality, higher morbidity and smoking-related accidents. Health care costs attributable to smoking are the result of self-damage by (primary) smokers or damage caused to non-smokers, environmental tobacco smoke. **The former includes early mortality of smokers, worse state of health of smokers than non-smokers and fire damage caused by smokers' negligence....**" (39)

Tobacco's latest marketing efforts produced global outrage, summed up perfectly in this comment "Tobacco companies used to deny that cigarettes killed people. Now they brag about it." (40)

"...In calculating savings in pensions and housing for the elderly, we considered that the saving of a smoker dying prematurely arises in the year of death. However, this is only one part of the positive effect." *Public Finance Balance of Smoking in the Czech Republic,* **Arthur D. Little International, Inc. report commissioned by Philip Morris, October 21, 1992**

Tobacco Sponsorship

Millions are budgeted by tobacco every year in Canada and elsewhere to sponsor jazz festivals (DuMaurier), Indy Races (Player's), tennis tournaments (Player's), fashion shows (Matinee), golf tournaments (Export A), fireworks displays (Benson & Hedges) - and even university grants, when they are accepted (University of Edmonton, Harvard refused). Tobacco sponsorship in Canada has been phased out. Contrary to the voice of doom predictions that without tobacco sponsorship, tourist attractions such as the Symphony of Fire event combining international fireworks display and music on the beach would not be able to take place, alternate sponsors have been found and nobody misses tobacco. Not even a little bit. (41)

Tobacco sponsorship of community and sporting events remains the last door open to gather public support, media and political allies in the promotion of a product whose sole use results in addiction and disease. Community by community, that door has slammed shut. Change takes time. The time has arrived.

"To have a health network headed by a tobacco executive brings a new meaning to the word 'hypocrisy'. (Ed Sweda, senior attorney

with Tobacco Products Liability Project in Boston. Philip Morris
board member Rupert Murdoch 's Fox Entertainment Group announced it will merge with American Health Network to launch a
new web-cable property called the Health Network, *Fox Gets
Healthy (But Keeps Smoking) The Industry Standard*, May 27, 1999

Summary

Big Tobacco struggle with creating the illusion implying they qualify as
members of industry who can claim corporate responsibility. They spare
no expense to build an image they believe will continue to hoodwink the
uninformed. Their polished public relations firm pride themselves in their
ability to create advocacy groups ostensibly comprised of Mr. & Mrs.
Average Citizen, when in reality membership consists of carefully chosen and well paid leaders to incite smokers and tobacco supporters in
protest against clean indoor air. Allegedly dispassionate scientific research, also tobacco-funded, surfaces regularly to dispute scientific data
originating from well-established medical and scientific sources of integrity. Tobacco-fronted business groups claiming to represent the interests of independent enterprise and the hospitality industry have only one
agenda: to resist any efforts restricting sales and consumption of tobacco.
Often separate groups reveal they represent only one organization, and
to maintain low overheads they operate from the same address. When
exposed, they simply re-register under yet another name.
     Expert witnesses are nothing new in trials; tobacco makes sure their
witnesses receive careful coaching (referred to as "developing") in
which lies about industry deception must be avoided and deflected
while testifying under oath. The phrase *safe cigarette* does not exist in
tobacco vocabulary; to imply research to create a *safe cigarette* admits
existing products are unsafe.
     Philip Morris have a history of denial repeatedly rejecting any suggestion
that consumption of their tobacco products results in suffering and premature death. In their desperate attempt to convince the government of Czechoslovakia to veto a bid to raise tobacco taxes, they commissioned a report
concluding smokers die early, and therefore save the government considerable money each year in old age pensions, housing and medical care.
     Dead smokers do not require income, a place to live or hospital treatment:
one reason Philip Morris presented to the Czechoslovakian government to
keep tobacco taxes low and tobacco consumption as high as possible.

• CHAPTER VII - THE BEGINNING OF THE END •
Smoking Bans and First Legal Victories Against Big Tobacco

"If we do not act decisively today, a hundred years from now our grandchildren and their children will look back and seriously question how people claiming to be committed to public health and social justice allowed the tobacco epidemic to unfold unchecked." *(Dr. Gro Harlem Brundtland, Director General, World Health Organization, November 14, 1999)*

The end of an era has to begin somewhere.

Smoking no longer enjoys the status it once did, as a socially acceptable consumer choice. Smoking tobacco has been identified for what it is: the vehicle of delivery for nicotine addiction. The by-product of setting tobacco products on fire, for the sole purpose of sucking smoke directly into the lungs, has been correctly identified as second-hand smoke, and has been irrefutably proven to cause lung cancer, emphysema and heart disease in nonsmokers involuntarily exposed to it. Tobacco has rightfully earned itself the reputation of an addict's option to send up in smoke hard-earned disposable income. Tobacco can now claim to kill more of the world's population every year than HIV, TB, childbirth, car accidents, alcohol abuse, drug abuse, fires, suicide and homicide - combined. (1) Tobacco can take a bow as the leading preventable cause of death around the world. (2)

Change takes time, and the beginning of the end of tobacco's glory days began half a century ago. Change has been gradual and hard-won every baby step of the way. But it has been won, and with each successful challenge to the tobacco industry, the world becomes one step closer to smoke-free. Change has arrived packaged in legal victories, legislated restrictions on where tobacco smoke may be produced, improved standards of occupational health and safety and public education and awareness programs resulting in decreased levels of smoking in direct proportion to education levels.

"The World Health Organization estimates that approximately 700 million, or almost half, of the world's children are exposed to second-hand smoke. In spite of what science tells us, however, in many places it is considered so acceptable to smoke, and so rude and unaccommodating to protest, that we dare not speak out against

second-hand smoke. The time has come for us to speak out. (Dr.
Gro Harlem Brundtland, Director General, World Health Organization. World No-Tobacco Day, May 31, 2001)

Early Tobacco Justice

Tobacco litigation's first significant cases appeared in the 1950's when
smokers who contracted lung, throat and laryngeal cancer attempted to
hold the tobacco industry liable for neglecting to declare the health
hazards caused by the use of their product. The Missouri lawsuit
brought against Philip Morris by a factory worker who lost his larynx
to cancer from smoking began the ongoing relationship between tobacco goliath Philip Morris and lawyers at Shook, Hardy, Bacon. Its
outcome set the pace for decades to come, when following one hour of
deliberation, the jury decided against the plaintiff, and tobacco began a
series of victories in the courtroom. Infinite financial resources to finance high-powered lawyers whose entire careers do not extend beyond defending tobacco against charges of negligence and fraud guaranteed tobacco courtroom victories for many years.

In a Pittsburgh, Pennsylvania courtroom in 1962, a jury determined
that plaintiff Otto Pritchard's lung cancer was caused by smoking; however, they found that Liggett & Myers Tobacco was not liable for his
death. (3) Tobacco rode the crest of the wave of courtroom victories
for approximately another quarter of a century. No lawsuit brought
against them could compete fairly with their legions of lawyers and the
one most important aspect unavailable to plaintiffs terminally ill with
lung cancer from smoking: time. Tobacco banked on this, literally, and
used every possible legal avenue open to them to delay litigation until
plaintiffs ran out of money, or time – or both.

In December, 1985 R. J. Reynolds won a product-liability suit
brought against them by the family of John M. Galbraith, a California
smoker who died not only of lung cancer, but emphysema and heart
disease. The Santa Barbara jury found the cigarette manufacturer not
liable for Mr. Galbraith's death.

In 1983 Rose Cipollone, 57, sued three tobacco companies as the
lung cancer she had from smoking ran its deadly course. Philip Morris,
Lorillard and Liggett Group claimed no responsibility for her illness,
although for 41 years she had daily smoked a pack and a half of the
cigarettes they produced. She claimed all three had failed to warn her

of the addictive nature of their product and the consequences to her health for using it as directed.

In compliance with the tobacco cartel strategy, tobacco lawyers delayed proceedings for eleven years. Mrs. Cipollone died in 1984 before her case could be heard in court. However, her lawyer pursued the case and broke new ground in a partial victory. District Court Judge Lee Sarokin ruled the discovery process should include disclosure of previously secret tobacco documents; this is the first lawsuit to deliver previously confidential corporate files and turn them over to courts of law and subsequent public records.

Judge Sarokin's ruling that Liggett pay Mrs. Cipollone's grieving family $400,000 in damages was the first time a tobacco company had been held liable for a smoker's death. The ruling stated Liggett Tobacco to be negligent for failing to warn smokers adequately prior to 1966. Philip Morris and Lorillard were completely exonerated because Mrs. Cipollone had started smoking their brands after 1966, after package warnings had appeared.

The ruling was overturned on a technicality and the Cipollone family dropped the lawsuit.

Cigarette package warnings have never appeared courtesy of the good intentions of the tobacco industry, who fought fiercely to avoid any warnings at all. To this day, any information on tobacco packaging outlining the consequences of its use appears there because the govenment puts it there. Tobacco has never voluntarily agreed to health warnings of any kind about its products.

"There was evidence starting to build in our own work that there was a connection. They had demonstrated emphysema in rabbits that had been exposed to cigarette smoke as defined by a clinical pathologist...My supervisor came in and asked that we turn in all our laboratory note books.. They contained all our experiments, our results. The explanation given was that the legal department wanted to see if there was something potentially dangerous to the company." Joseph Bumgarner, biochemist, formerly employed by R. J. Reynolds Tobacco, quoted in *Tobacco Wars*, a BBC documentary on history and politics of tobacco broadcast July/August 1999

When Susan Haines sued R.J. Reynolds Tobacco Co., Lorillard Tobacco Co., and Philip Morris Inc. for the wrongful death of her father, the door opened to public disclosure of confidential tobacco documents. Susan Haines' attorney argued successfully that the Council for Tobacco Research documents had established a distinct division wherein documents damaging to tobacco's image remained safely stored with tobacco attorneys, protected by attorney/client privilege. Meanwhile only evidence supporting the tobacco cartel's claims about the safety of their products would be released for public consumption. Susan Haines' attorney further argued these documents did not warrant protection under attorney/client privilege because of the "crime/fraud exception". This means client privilege is waived when the client obtained legal advice for the purpose of perpetuating ongoing criminal and/or fraudulent crimes. Susan Haines' attorney argued successfully the Council for Tobacco Research Group had a clear mandate to conceal from the public the evidence they had confirming the harmful effects of smoking.

In February 1992, Judge Sarokin (the same judge in the Cipollone case) ruled the "crime/fraud exception" applied to some of the documents he had reviewed, and quoted excerpts of the more incriminating papers. "No evidence could be more damning" he ruled, when he read aloud the minutes of a 1981 meeting with tobacco lawyers, repeating the words of one of the attendees who said *"When we started the CTR [Council for Tobacco Research] Special Projects, the idea was that the scientific director of CTR would review a project. If he liked it, it was a CTR special project. If he did not like it, then it became a lawyers' special project.... We wanted to protect it under the lawyers. We did not want it out in the open."* (4)

Flight Attendants Initiate the Momentum

In October 1997, an American Airlines flight attendant named Norma Broin took the courtroom tobacco battles to the next level: class action litigation. Norma Broin had never smoked or been exposed to tobacco smoke until she began working as a flight attendant. The usual alibis (caffeine, alcohol) for causing cancer presented by the tobacco cartel did not apply to Norma Broin, who was born and raised a Mormon. At the age of 35, fourteen years into her career as a flight attendant working in smoky airline cabins, Norma Broin received the devastating diagnosis of lung cancer. She led the class-action suit of 60,000 non-smoking flight attendants exposed to cigarette smoke in their workplace and won damages of $349 million, in addition to tobacco's grudging agreement to support smoke-free regulations on international flights. The award directed $300 million to open the Broin Research Foundation whose mandate would be to study diseases caused by smoking. Predictably tobacco appealed this decision and the ruling was upheld in this, the first class-action suit against tobacco in the United States. The 60,000 flight attendants received no financial compensation; however, the victory entitled them to file individual suits. (5) The verdict meant tobacco must prove exposure to secondhand smoke did not cause ailments claimed by each of the flight attendants.

"Those gas-permeable contact lenses, oh yeah, they turned yellow. Your eyes would sting, you'd have headaches, your chest would burn, You would ask the captain to turn the 'No Smoking' sign on for a while so that people would stop smoking. We would actually go up in the cockpit and use some of the pilot's oxygen" (Norma Broin, American Airlines Flight Attendant, describing the conditions of occupational health and safety of her workplace, aboard an aircraft with smoking passengers, May 29, 1997, Reuters)

Minnesota Paves the Way

January, 1998 saw the dawn of another new age of tobacco litigation. On behalf of Minnesota State,   Minnesota Attorney General Hubert Humphrey III and Chief Executive Officer of Blue Cross and Blue Shield (Minnesota) Andrew Czajkowski brought a lawsuit against the tobacco industry. The defendants named in the suit were Philip Morris, R.J. Reynolds, Brown & Williamson, Lorillard, Liggett Group, The Tobacco Institute/Council for Tobacco Research – U.S.A. The claims against them alleged consumer fraud, deceptive trade practices, unlawful trade practices, false advertising, antitrust conspiracy and breach of duty to public (Minnesota State only). The antitrust conspiracy included the claim that the tobacco industry controlled the market for cigarettes through its deliberate conspiracy to conceal the truth about them.

In the Minnesota Trial, a judge ruled tobacco documents did not qualify for consideration of client/attorney privilege because they contained evidence of crime and fraud. Eight hundred tobacco documents became publicly available over the internet and were given the nickname "Bliley documents", after House Commerce Committee Chairman U. S. Rep. Tom Bliley. He subpoenaed the documents from Philip Morris, RJR Nabisco, Lorillard and Brown & Williamson when they refused to turn them over voluntarily.

Judge Kenneth Fitzpatrick set new precedents for tobacco litigation and paved the way for others to hold tobacco accountable for their fraud in courts of law throughout the U.S. He ordered the establishment of tobacco document depositories, which now contain 33 million pages of previously confidential tobacco research documents, letters and internal memoranda. Just over four months into the trial, a settlement was reached. Tobacco agreed to pay the plaintiffs $6 billion over twenty-five years, to include not only recovery for the cost of treating illness caused by smoking, but punitive damages. $1.7 billion had been the original claim. (6)

Victory in Florida

In this precedent-setting class action suit against tobacco, Miami pediatrician Howard Engle became the name associated with the first class action lawsuit against tobacco to get to trial in the history of the U.S. The tobacco cartel had successfully blocked twenty-four previous efforts. (7)

Angie Della Vechhia, 53, one of the lead plaintiffs, was scheduled to testify how she had smoked for forty years and the tobacco industry concealed the information they knew about the addictiveness of nicotine and the health consequences of smoking. She never had her day in court. A year after being told her lung cancer had spread to her brain, she died.

157 witnesses testified during the Engle trial, over a period of two years. After four hours of deliberation, the jury awarded $145 billion to the plaintiffs. In addition to the substantial punitive and compensatory damages, the historic victory over tobacco fraud and deception wrote another volume for the growing library of lawsuits succesfully holding them accountable for their lack of ethics, morals and decency.

"We commend the Engle jurors for their courage and wisdom. When the dirty secrets of tobacco were forced into the light of day in a public courtroom, six average Americans saw the truth. Their resounding verdict sends a message to Big Tobacco on behalf of all Americans that cannot be ignored: We will hold you accountable

for your misdeeds and you won't get away with it again." **John R. Seffrin, Ph.D, Chief Executive Officer of the American Cancer Society. July 14, 2000 . American Cancer Society, Florida** *Join The Fight*

Started Smoking at 13

Richard Boeken, started smoking 43 years ago. He quit in 1997 when he received the news he had lung cancer. He learned the lung cancer had spread to his brain, and his name become linked to the first smoking and health case ever tried in Los Angeles County. In June, 2001, a jury awarded him $5.54 million in compensatory and $3 billion in punitive damages, the biggest verdict to date for individual damages. This victory marked the seventh defeat for tobacco in 23 jury verdicts since February of 1999 – a 30% success rate and hard-earned legal precedents. However, no amount of damages or success rates in the courtroom could restore Mr. Boeken's health, ruined forever by a product whose manufacturer lied and denied for so long. At the age of 57, Mr. Boeken died of lung cancer on January 16, 2002. Philip Morris continue to appeal the award.

Thanks to pioneer plaintiffs who tackled the monstrous tobacco industry, precedents have been set to demand accountability for the safety of products manufactured by tobacco. The "contributory negligence" defense favored by tobacco's slick lawyers became less of an option when the evidence could no longer be denied that tobacco knew about the harm caused by their product and deliberately lied. Strict liability evolved over the years, meaning tobacco could be found liable for damages.

Smoking Restrictions Become the New Social Norm

Arizona can take credit for being the first state in the U.S. to restrict smoking in some public buildings on August 8, 1973. San Francisco became the first city in the U.S. implementing restrictive laws about workplace smoking on June 3, 1983.

A sign in Los Angeles airport welcomes travellers to California: The Non Smoking Section of America. California leads the way with some of the tightest restrictions on smoking in the world. All workplaces in California are smoke-free and contrary to the prediction of doom by the tobacco cartel, California's tourist industry has not died, the hospitality industry is thriving, movie theatres remain profitable and the public flocks to restaurants and bars as much (and more in some instances) as ever.

Reducing tobacco consumption results when social norms change. Fifty years ago, smoking was considered acceptable. Steadily, smoking has become reviled for the filthy pastime it's always been. The future of tobacco reduction rests with today's youth, who do not like being taken for fools by an industry who sees them through a profit viewfinder.

"Imagine a five-year old child, who will be a future customer of your cigarettes in the next few years. How can your company begin to attract/tap into this next generation? Flanigan Enterprises is proposing a children's video be made to advertise the Camel product...Children love to watch animals (repeatability) and this video can incorporate an education/environment theme. How often smokers are told, 'it is a bad example for children in our home to see you smoke.' Here is a positive way to enhance the image of R.J. Reynolds in the home — to engrain a positive image of the company to the children of the non-smoker while linking the video to purchase of cigarettes. "December 9, 1988 letter from Flanigan Enterprises to R. J. Reynolds Tobacco. Bates Number 513612438

Summary

Tobacco's days have always been numbered, linked closely to the reduced span of a smoker's lifetime. Concealing information about the health consequences of smoking becomes increasingly difficult as smokers die by the hundreds of thousands every year in North America.

Early tobacco litigation resulted in defeat for the victims of tobacco's deception. Tobacco have grown accustomed to buying their way to victory and gradually that trend has shifted. Not all judges can be bought and paid for with tobacco blood money; not all jurors believe tobacco lies anymore. A Florida jury sent a clear message to tobacco in the only way tobacco understands: the largest punitive damages ever awarded against any corporation, $145 billion.

The message left no doubt that the lies will no longer be tolerated.

• VIII - MILLIONS FOR BILLIONS •
Millions Die for Billions in Tobacco Profits

"Imperial Tobacco [Canada] sold 32.8 billion cigarettes (and equivalent) in 2000 Profit per cigarette for the year 2001 = $0.031" (*Profits per Cigarette* **Physicians for a Smoke-Free Canada)**

The earliest recorded research into the fatal qualities of tobacco appears when Samuel Pepys writes in 1665 about a laboratory experiment in which an unfortunate cat was fed drops of "distilled oil of tobacco", and died. In 1761 London physician Dr. John Hill performed perhaps the first clinical study of tobacco effects, warning snuff users that they are increasing their risk of nasal cancer. In 1795 Sammuel Thomas von Soemmering of Maine reports on cancers of the lip in pipe smokers and in 1798 Dr. Benjamin Rush, a U.S. Founding Father, wrote on the medical dangers of tobacco and claims that smoking or chewing tobacco leads to drunkenness.

One of the earliest medical records about health consequences of tobacco use appeared in 1859. Hospital records show 68 patients in Montpellier, France who had cancer of the lips, tongue, tonsils and other parts of the mouth. All, without exception, used tobacco. 66 of them smoked short-stemmed clay pipes. This type of pipe became unpopular following the release of this information although it remained in use by smokers who then, as now, typically believe tobacco consumption makes only other people sick.

An estimated 62 million Americans were current smokers in 1996. This represents a smoking rate of 29 percent for the population age 12 and older. There was no change between 1995 and 1996 overall. Current smokers are more likely to be heavy drinkers and illicit drug users. Among smokers, the rate of heavy alcohol use (five or more drinks on five or more days in the past month) was 12.8 percent, and the rate of current illicit drug use was 14.7 percent. Among nonsmokers, only 2.5 percent were heavy drinkers and 2.6 percent were illicit drug users. An estimated 6.8 million Americans (3.2 percent of the population) were current users of smokeless tobacco in 1996. The rate has not changed since 1993. Tobacco use remains the leading preventable cause of death in the United States, causing more than 400,000 deaths and $50 billion in direct medical costs each year. (1)

Smoking and the military have a long partnership. American outcome

of World War I, according to General John J. Pershing, depended on tobacco rations for G.I.'s. "Gen. John J. Pershing wrote: "You ask what we
need to win this war. I answer tobacco as much as bullets. Tobacco is as the
daily ration; we must have thousands of tons without delay."

    Although the science of nicotine addiction was not yet clearly un-
derstood, military leaders knew that a buzz of nicotine provided brief
respite from the rigors of war and free cigarettes became an integral part
of soldiers' C-rations. Nonsmoking soldiers who enlisted to serve their
country came home from Europe firmly addicted to nicotine, giving another sinister meaning to the phrase *prisoner of war.* Allied soldiers had
acquired a deadly enemy, in addition to Hitler and his nazis. The tobacco
industry gave a new meaning to the word "traitor". Simple arithmetic
clearly indicates more soldiers were killed during the Second World War
from tobacco use than enemy fire. Who was the real enemy?

**"For decades the Pentagon (apparently, with congressional approval)
put cigarettes in GIs' C-rations, helping young soldiers get addicted
to tobacco."** *"Military Right To End Killer Tobacco Subsidy,"* **SAN
ANTONIO EXPRESS-NEWS, October 24, 1996, p. B4. (sdb 11/1/96)**

"I Shall Return": tobacco capitalizes on a truly captive audience

Tobacco adopted General Douglas MacArthur's "I Shall Return" war-
time promise as the brand name for cigarettes smuggled behind enemy
lines and dropped at night from B-24 bombers to the Japanese-occu-
pied Philippines. (2)
Larus & Bro Tobacco Company had been awarded the contract to provide
cigarettes in soldiers' C-rations during World War II. In a secure area of
their cigarette factory, they assembled small packages containing four cigarettes each, in an operation classified as top secret by the Office of War
Information. Together with sewing kits, *I Shall Return* matches, match-
boxes and reflectors (for signaling aircraft), Chelsea cigarettes were distributed in occupied territory by U.S. and Filipino guerrillas.
    Each package boasted General MacArthur's signature and the hope
of liberation. Enslavement to nicotine addiction inevitably followed.
    Tobacco products sold in military canteens at discounted prices of
20% - 60% less than civilian outlets encouraged continuation of nicotine addiction and anyone who protested could find themselves labelled
a traitor. The effects of tobacco take a decade or two before they be-

This brand of cigarettes appeared in a 1950's movie *An American Guerrilla in the Philippines* as instrumental in defeating the Japanese army. In one scene, a Filipino peasant caught smoking this brand was executed for treason by a Japanese soldier.

come apparent, and can last for an additional decade or two or three before they cause death. In WWII, U.S. military losses included 292,131 battle deaths and 115,187 other deaths. More Americans die each year from tobacco consumption than the soldiers who died in combat during the entire Second World War. (3)

The U.S. military has drastically altered its policy on smoking, discouraging ever starting and providing support for those who want to quit; however, 58 million cartons of cigarettes continue to be sold each year through military commissaries. In 1986, Defense Secretary Caspar Weinberger overruled a decision by his assistant secretary for health affairs to eliminate discount on cigarettes purchase in military stores. Military groups had protested that this would provide a "dangerous precedent" for cuts in other benefits. Then Surgeon-General C. Everett Koop commented, "How could this be viewed as a reduction in benefits, when the only benefits would be a lifetime of illness and early death?"

Smoking and Health – The Consequences

➤ Each year, smoking kills more people than AIDS, alcohol abuse, drug abuse, car crashes, murders, suicides and fires – combined. (4)
➤ 90% of lung cancer occurs in smokers or people who have smoked (5)
➤ 85% of lung cancer occurs in smokers and ex-smokers (6)
➤ 85%-90% of lung cancers are the direct result of smoking (7)
➤ Among smokers age 35 to 69 smoking accounts for a three fold increase in the death rate, and approximately half of all regular smokers

that begin smoking during adolescence will be killed by tobacco. (8)

➤ Bruce Leistikow, Professor of Epidemiology and Preventive Medicine at the University of California-Davis, published research in June 2001 about the numbers of children under the age of 18 who qualify for social assistance payments because their fathers died from diseases caused by smoking. They receive $1.5 billion per year from the government in Social Security Survivor's Insurance.

➤ Smokers make greater use of inpatient and outpatient hospital services and lower use of preventive care services (9).

➤ The relative risk of a smoker developing Coronary Artery Disease or myocardial infarction is 1.7 to that of never smokers. (10)

➤ Smokers have 33% more angina per day than non-smokers. Furthermore, in patients continuing to smoke within 3 weeks of receiving thrombolytic therapy after a myocardial infarction the risk of reinfarction increased from 5.1% to 20% compared to smokers who quit. (11).

➤ Between 50% to 55% of all strokes in the United States are directly attributable to cigarette smoking. A smoker is 1.5 to 3 times more likely to develop cerebrovascular disease. (12)

➤ Smoking more than 15 cigarettes per day more than doubles the rate of limb amputation after revascularization as compared to those of never smokers. (13)

➤ 59% of all aortic aneurysm is secondary to smoking. The death risk of AAA is two to three times higher in smokers as compared to never smokers. (14)

➤ Because of cigarette smoking patterns over the last several decades, lung cancer has surpassed breast cancer as the leading cause of cancer death in women since 1987. (15)

➤ Smoking is the major cause of lung cancer. The risk of developing laryngeal cancer is approximately 10 fold greater for a male and 8 fold greater for a female as compared to never smokers (16)

➤ Smoking is a major cause of oral cancer, accounting for 92% of these cancers in men and 61% in women. The increased risk attributed to smoking is of 27 fold in men and 6 fold in women. (17)

➤ Nearly 80% of all deaths from esophageal cancer are attributable to cigarette smoking. Smokers have a 8 to 10 fold greater risk of developing esophageal cancer than nonsmokers. (18)

➤ Close to 50% of all bladder and kidney cancer deaths in men are caused by smoking. The risk of developing these cancers is two to three times greater for both male and female smokers than that of

the nonsmoking population. (19)
➤ There is approximately a twofold increase in the risk of developing pancreatic cancer with smoking and this risk is dose dependent. (20)
➤ There is approximately a 50% increase in the risk of stomach cancer in smokers compared to never smokers. (21)
➤ All exposure to tobacco smoke is exceedingly detrimental to babies, both born and unborn. Studies have confirmed that smoking increases the rate of low birth weight babies, premature babies, spontaneous abortions, stillbirths, neonatal death, abruptio placentae, placenta previa, bleeding during pregnancy, prolonged rupture of membranes, and impaired development of the infant. This can be attributed to several factors such as the vasoconstriction of placenta blood flow by nicotine, elevated fetal carboxyhemoglobin and catecholamine levels, fetal tissue hypoxia, reduced delivery of nutrients to the fetus, and increased heart rate and blood pressure (22)
➤ Smoking is associated with the development, delayed healing and recurrence of peptic ulcer, as well as resistance to treatment. (23)
➤ Smoking is a risk factor for osteoporosis and bone fractures. (24)

"We don't believe it's ever been established that smoking is the cause of disease." Walker Merryman, vice-president and chief spokesman for the Tobacco Institute, testifying at the Minnesota trial Feb 1998

Formal Research Completed About Additional Aspects of Smoking

➤ Alcoholics are more likely to die from the effects of smoking than from those of alcohol. (25)
➤ Alcoholism is ten times more likely among smokers than among nonsmokers. Possible explanations for this include a susceptibility on the part of some individuals to addictive drugs in general, and/ or for some individuals tobacco smoking and alcoholism are both sequelae of a propensity to behave irresponsibly. (26)
➤ People with a diagnosable mental disorder consume nearly half of all cigarettes smoked in the United States. (27)

"With millions of Americans dead from lung cancer who were smokers, I have no reason to ask for proof from animals." Dr. Jonathan Samet, cancer specialist, Johns Hopkins University, sworn testimony at the Minnesota trial

Smoking and Blindness

Women smoking 25 or more cigarettes a day had 2.4 times the risk of developing sight impairment. Women with a history of smoking had a twofold increased risk of macular degeneration, with little drop in risk even in those who had stopped smoking more than 15 years before (28)

Direct Link Between Smoking and Lung Cancer Explained Beyond Doubt

Tobacco's constant denial that the connection has never been proven between smoking and lung cancer can no longer be claimed. The tobacco incantation that they are in the nicotine delivery business with tar as the negative baggage has a firm foundation of truth.

"Tar" refers to the particulate matter inherent in cigarette smoke when tobacco is burned. Each particle contains organic and inorganic chemicals. Tar takes credit for those yellow smoke-stained teeth and fingers when it becomes a sticky-brown substance in its condensate form . Not all tar remains permanently in the lungs. Some gets coughed up when smokers have their morning clear-out as their lungs make their futile attempt to cleanse themselves. Some gets exhaled. The tar that remains in the lungs sticks to the *cilia*, very fine, tiny hairs that line the airways to act as a filter against bacteria and airborne pollution. Cigarette tar destroys and paralyzes the cilia. When their natural cleansing process is impeded, tar travels deeper into the lungs where it converts healthy, pink and sponge-like lung tissue into blackened, charred and inefficient breathing apparatus.

A pack a day smoker inhales a quart of thick, gooey, brownish black tar directly into their lungs every year. (29)

Benzo(a)pyrene is a component of tar contained in tobacco smoke. Benzo(a)pyrene causes cancer in animals and fish in every study to date. (30)

In 1996 biochemist Dr. Moon Shon-Tang at the M.D. Anderson Cancer Centre in Houston confirmed that tobacco smoke exposure results in mutation of a tumor-suppressing gene known as P53. When healthy, this gene acts to control potentially dangerous and malignant cells and prevent them from reproducing and spreading throughout the body. When damaged, this gene becomes ineffective and cell division is no longer regulated or kept in check. Dr. Tang and his associates reported that about 60% of human lung cancers contain mutations in the tumor suppressor gene P53.

Dr. Kenneth Olden, Director of the Federal National Institute of Environmental Health Sciences in Triangle Park, N.C., said "It's an exciting finding. Much of the evidence we have that smoking causes lung cancer is circumstantial, although extremely strong. It's really good to have some more definitive evidence to support it". (31)

Women and Smoking

" ... **Women smokers are likely to increase as a percentage of the total. Women are adopting more dominant roles in society: they have increased spending power, they live longer than men. As a recent official report showed, they seem to be less influenced by the anti-smoking campaigns than their male counterparts...All in all, that makes women a prime target as far as any alert European marketing man is concerned. So, despite previous hesitancy, might we now expect to see a more defined attack on the important market segment defined by female smokers?"** (32)

Because particulates in cigarette smoke can harm machinery and electronic equipment, Philip Morris prohibits smoking in its plants around the machines it uses to manufacture 900,000,000 cigarettes every day. Smoking is prohibited in tobacco greenhouses, because tobacco smoke harms and stunts the growth of tender tobacco seedlings. Corporate responsibility for the efficient and profitable manufacture of cigarettes does not extend to concern for public health, because the tobacco industry strenuously resists any efforts to restrict smoking in workplaces and public buildings. Tobacco seedlings apparently take precedence over human health and life.

The devastating consequences of tobacco use have no gender preference. Women, however, have become a more vulnerable tobacco target than their male counterparts for four reasons.

"However, recent studies have shown that as women's smoking habits become more like men's, women smokers become more prone to the same illnesses as male smokers." Lorillard Tobacco internal memorandum June 28, 1973, Bates Number 03375503

Firstly, by marketing tobacco products with names like *Virginia Slims* the tobacco industry appeal to a universal fear women have: weight gain. Nicotine consumption can artificially increase metabolism in some women and the tobacco cartel's marketing efforts capitalize on this side-effect to create the image of a typical female smoker who is pencil slim, glamorous and sexy. Tobacco advertisements never talk about the dramatic weight loss that occurs when lung cancer sets in. Super model Christy Turlington, admits she smoked for ten years to help with weight control. At age 28, she was diagnosed with emphysema. Her father, a smoker, died of lung cancer.

The Dieticians of Canada confirm a weight gain of 80 to 100 lbs. would be necessary to offset the benefits of quitting smoking. Weight gain of 5 – 10 lbs. following smoking cessation can be reversed within a month or two and the health benefits of quitting smoking last a lifetime.

Secondly, coronary heart disease, usually considered to be a male concern, in reality is equally serious for women. Within one minute of inhaling tobacco smoke, the heart rate begins to rise and can increase as much as 30% in ten minutes. When the carbon monoxide in tobacco smoke is absorbed into the bloodstream, it displaces oxygen and thereby reduces the quantity of oxygen that reaches the heart. Oxygen depletion causes the heart to work harder that normal. Smokers have raised fibrinogen levels and platelet counts, and tobacco smoke also increases the tendency of blood platelets to stick together, thus increasing the chances of a blood clot forming in a major coronary artery, and blocking blood flow to the heart. Sudden blockage of an artery can result in a fatal heart attack, a stroke, or gangrene of the leg.

Tobacco smoke lowers the "good" cholesterol (high density lipoprotein) in the arteries, and damages artery linings, resulting in an accumulated build-up of calcium deposits on artery walls. These deposits restrict blood flow, and when they break away, damage to the heart or brain result. Bypass patients who continue to smoke completely cancel any benefits from expensive and major surgery. The waiting lists are long, and successful treatment depends on patient co-operation. Those smokers who claim they have the choice to smoke must also make the choice to die from heart disease when they refuse to quit. In Canada and Australia, doctors have refused surgery to patients who refuse to quit smoking.

Smoking by women in the United States causes nearly as many deaths from heart disease as from lung cancer. (33)

The third major reason women are singled out for increased risk of smoking-related disease involves use of oral contraceptives. The risk of coronary heart disease significantly increases among smoking women over their smoke-free counterparts. Smoking also decreases the effectiveness of oral contraception for some women.

The fourth and final consequence of smoking unique to women concerns pregnancy and breastfeeding. Because the carbon monoxide in tobacco smoke displaces oxygen in the bloodstream, a developing fetus becomes oxygen deprived every time the mother smokes. A higher rate of low birthweight babies, premature births, stillbirths and infant mortality exists among women who smoke while pregnant. Many factors contribute to the tragedy of SIDS (Sudden Infant Death Syndrome) and one of the avoidable risks is smoking. Exposure to tobacco smoke, both *in utero* before birth and after delivery, increases the possibility a baby will die of SIDS.

Cornell University and the University of Rochester conducted research concluding lower I.Q. scores exist for babies whose mothers smoked. Smoking mothers inhale carbon monoxide and nicotine, both of which reach the baby via the placenta and prevent it from obtaining adequate oxygen and nutrients. Smoking mothers who breastfeed provide their babies with nicotine-laced milk and in extreme cases, the babies suffer nicotine withdrawal between feeds.

Research Midwife Ah Fong Hoo of the Institute of Child Health and Great Ormond Street Hospital in London, England specializes in research into factors influencing prenatal and neonatal growth and development of the lungs. She and her team found that maternal smoking retards and damages the structure of fetal lungs and airways. Prenatal exposure to nicotine results in changes to the nervous system resulting in impaired breathing.

Smoking and Birth Defects

➢ Cigarette smoking can cause reproductive problems before a woman even becomes pregnant. Women at greatest risk for fertility problems are those who smoke one or more packs a day, and started smoking before the age of 18. (Smoking also causes changes in a man's sperm that may reduce his fertility.) (33)

➢ Women who smoke early in pregnancy double their risk of having an ectopic pregnancy, in which the embryo becomes implanted in a fallopian tube or other abnormal site instead of the uterus. These pregnancies rarely result in the birth of a baby, and must be removed surgically or with drug treatment to protect a woman's life. Ectopic pregnancy remains an important cause of maternal deaths in parts of the world where these treatments are not readily available. (34)

➤ Smokers are up to 80 percent more likely to suffer a miscarriage than their non-smoking counterparts. They are also twice as likely to develop potentially life-threatening placental complications resulting in a delivery that jeopardizes the life of mother and baby. Placental problems contribute to smokers' increased risk of having a stillborn baby. (35)

➤ Smoking nearly doubles a woman's risk of having a low birthweight baby. Low birthweight babies, who weigh less than 5 ½ pounds at birth, face an increased risk of serious health problems during the newborn period, chronic disabilities (such as cerebral palsy, mental retardation and learning problems), and even death. (36)

➤ It's also important to stay smoke-free after the baby is born. Babies who are exposed to smoke suffer from more respiratory illnesses and ear infections than other babies. For example, infants whose mothers smoke are 38 percent more likely to be hospitalized for pneumonia during their first year of life than babies of non-smoking mothers. Smoking in the home during the first few years of a child's life also increases his risk of developing asthma.

➤ Women who smoke may pass genetic mutations that increase cancer risks, including leukemia, to their children. Smoking by fathers prior to conception can increase the risk of childhood cancers and mental retardation , even when the mother does not smoke. (37)

➤ Pregnant women who smoke will significantly increase the risk of their children being born mentally retarded and/or developing behavioral problems. (38)

➤ Women who smoke are more likely to have babies with cleft lip or palate. (39)

➤ Aggressive marketing to attract women smokers has resulted in lung cancer overtaking breast cancer as the leading cause of cancer deaths among American women . Since 1960, lung cancer mortality rates for women have increased 600%. (40)

"Cigarette packs frequently held in a brightly nail-polished hand against a background of flower/plants or in traditional feminine hobby situations...This traditional and very feminine approach...is

directed to the woman whose life revolves around her role as a women, being pretty, soft, and feminine and gaining fulfillment from acceptably female hobbies. Even the promotion offered, a horoscope, exemplifies women's passivity and lack of control over her own future." Lorillard Tobacco Company Internal Memorandum June 28, 1973 Bates Number 03375503

Tobacco: A Global Pandemic

Every death caused by tobacco is 100% preventable.

In 1998, four million deaths were attributable to tobacco use globally. If present smoking patterns continue, especially in developing countries, by the year 2030 that number will rise to 10 million deaths annually - roughly equal to the current combined mortality from diarrhoeal diseases, malaria, pneumonia and tuberculosis. In developed countries, half of deaths caused by smoking will be in productive and socially important middle age from 35 to 69 years. (41)

Green Tobacco Sickness

A less well known tobacco-caused illness affects approximately 10% of tobacco farm workers. When moisture-covered tobacco plants are harvested, usually early morning or early evening, nicotine is absorbed through the skin of tobacco workers and causes illness. Effects manifest three to seventeen hours following exposure and last up to three days. They include nausea, dizziness, vomiting, abdominal cramps, headache, respiratory distress, increased perspiration and salivation, abnormal blood pressure and heart rate. (42)

Protective water-resistant clothing, gloves, boots and socks improve workplace safety for those who harvest the same plant the tobacco industry encourages its customers to set on fire in bars and restaurants, with no regard for the workplace safety of hospitality staff, who have no protective apparatus against the dangerous poison which is an integral part of tobacco products when they are set afire and use as intended.

Chemicals Found in Tobacco Smoke – Known Human Carcinogens:

4- Aminobiphenyl: No known safe level of this chemical exists. It is no longer produced on a commercial scale for use in industry. (43)

Benzene: Known to cause leukemia in humans. Benzene produces chromosomal aberrations in humans. (44)

Cadmium: Cadmium primarily targets the kidneys. Main industrial use of cadmium includes storage batteries, pigments and dry film lubricants. (45)

Chromium: Chromium compounds easily pass into human cells through cell membranes (by inhalation). (46)

2-Aminoapthylamine: Because it is known to cause cancer, the industrial use of this chemical is severely restricted or banned. (47)

Nickel: Nickel inhalation increases susceptibility to respiratory infection, pulmonary edema and cancer of the gastrointestinal system. The main uses of nickel in industry include production of stainless steel, alloys, electroplating, coinage and alkaline batteries. (48)

Polonium-210 (Radon): Cigarette smoke contains radioactive lead and polonium. Each cigarette smoked can be equated to one chest x-ray. (49)

Vinyl Chloride: Also known as chloroethene, chloroethylene, ethylene monochloride, and monochloroethylene, vinyl chloride is flammable as a gas and is not stable at high temperatures or pressure. Continued inhalation of vinyl chloride results in damage to the liver, the lungs and kidneys. If you spill liquid vinyl chloride on your skin, it will numb the skin and cause redness and blisters. (50)

Additional Chemicals Found in Tobacco Smoke

Arsenic When burned, it emits a garlic-like odor. Used as an insecticide.

Acetone Damages liver and kidneys; burns skin on direct contact.

Acrolein Long term inhalation causes emphysema, also inflammation of the lungs, liver and kidneys.

Acrylonitrile Withdrawn in the U.S. as a fumigant for all food commodities. Still used in tobacco.

Benzo[a]pyrene Exposure results in decreased reproductive capacity for males and females.

Carbon Monoxide Carbon Monoxide binds to haemoglobin, reducing the oxygen-carrying capacity of the blood.

Catechol When inhaled with benzo[a]pyrene, catechol is co-carcinogenic. Industrial uses include insecticides, inks, and dyes.

Crotonaldehyde Crotonaldehyde causes cancer by interfering with DNA function. This is known as a genotoxic carcinogen. Industrial use for crotonaldehyde is as a warning agent in fuel gases.

Cresol causes dermatitis in humans. Long term exposure causes nausea, vomiting, elevated blood pressure, impaired kidney function, and tremors. Main industrial uses include disinfectants, fumigants and explosives.

Formaldehyde Causes cellular changes in the upper respiratory tract and adversely affects the liver. Industrial uses include fertilizer, dyes, germicides and embalming fluid for human corpses.

Hydrogen Cyanide Causes nasal irritation, weakness and nausea. This is the "gas" used in nazi extermination camp gas chambers. Industrial use includes insecticides, electroplating and metallurgy.

Lead interacts with enzymes, especially those associated with blood Long term exposure to lead causes kidney disease, and led adversely affects sperm count. Industrial uses for lead include batteries and paint pigments.

Methyl Ethyl Ketone causes nose, throat and eye irritation. Industrial uses include solvents, artificial leather, rubbers, varnishes and glue.

Nitric Oxide reacts with haemoglobin to hinder oxygen uptake in the blood. When combined with carbon monoxide (also in tobacco smoke), the toxicity becomes cumulative.

Phenol damages the lungs and central nervous system, and can cause convulsions. Industrial uses include disinfectants, germicidal paints and slimicides.

Pyridine causes upper respiratory tract and eye irritation. Industrial use includes solvents, pesticides and resins.

Quinoline causes genetic mutations. Main industrial uses include insecticides, herbicides, corrosion inhibitors and preservation of pathology specimens.

Toluene appears in blood circulation within ten seconds, and accumulates in body fat. Long term low level exposure results in menstrual irregularities, reductions in cognitive and motor skills. Industrial use includes rubbers, adhesives, dyes and explosives.

Tobacco-Specific Nitrosamines NNN is a carcinogenic tobacco-specific nitrosamine found only in tobacco products, known to cause nose, throat, lung and digestive tract cancer in animals and reproductive damage in humans. NNK is a carcinogenic tobacco-specific nitrosamine found only in tobacco products and is a powerful lung carcinogen. NAT is a possibly carcinogenic tobacco-specific nitrosamine found only in tobacco products.

"The truth is that one out of every two long-term smokers will ultimately be killed by tobacco." World Health Organization Fact Sheet No 221, April 1999

Summary

An estimated 47 million adults smoke in the United States. One in two smokers will suffer, become debilitated by and die from tobacco-caused disease. (51)

Tobacco does not kill instantly and tobacco does not limit its devastation with only one disease per smoker. Individual smokers can and do acquire emphysema *and* lung cancer *and* heart disease, simultaneously. Emphysema takes years to kill, by slow suffocation. Lung cancer requires surgical removal of the affected area of each lung, radiation and chemotherapy. Sometimes these treatments eradicate the disease; there is no way of knowing whether it will return as the original tumor metastasizes (spreads) elsewhere, typically to the brain, bones, and liver. Smokers' circulation becomes so poor that fingers "club", which means that the tips of fingers become flattened. In some cases, amputation of feet and legs becomes necessary.

One in every five deaths is caused by tobacco consumption.

Not only smokers suffer; babies born to smoking mothers are at higher risk for pregnancy complications and birth defects. Fourteen people die each day in California as the result of exposure to second-hand smoke.

Three million people under the age of 18 smoke half a billion cigarettes a year. The Canadian tobacco industry enjoyed a profit of .026 cents per cigarette in the year 2000, and sold 32.8 billion cigarettes. (52) Those under the age of 18 may choose to smoke; they do not choose nicotine addiction . The tobacco cartel takes care of that aspect once they have sold the scam to teenagers that smoking is all that's required to appear "adult".

American smokers have consumed 17 trillion cigarettes (remember that profit per cigarette). Laid end to end, these would circle the planet at the equator 36,000 times. (53)

Under an agreement between Brown & Williamson Tobacco and the British government in 1997, 600 additives are permitted in cigarettes. They include arsenic, ammonia, chemicals used to make weed killer, car batteries, ant poison, paint stripper, lighter fuel and mothballs. These poisons included in each cigarette present additional danger when ignited, including production of forty carcinogens.

Not one of these additives or their by-products is listed on any package labelling for tobacco.

• IX - CIGARETTE LIGHTER SIDE •
Mouth Fires and Comical Tobacco Liars

There is nothing funny about nicotine addiction and the devastation caused by tobacco consumption. However, doctors such as Patch Adams believe in the power of laughter to heal and to help, and taking a look at some of the more comical claims made about tobacco can do no harm. Decades of denial and deception by the tobacco industry have on occasion been so absurd they have literally become jokes. Some of the funniest comments originate with tobacco industry executives who actually expected to be taken seriously when they said the following:

• Dr. Helmut Wakeham, a Philip Morris research scientist claimed in a 1970's documentary that eating too much applesauce is as dangerous as smoking.(1)

• James J. Morgan, CEO of Philip Morris Co. gave a sworn deposition in 1997 saying smoking was no more addictive than eating Gummi Bears candy. He retired just before the industry's massive defeat in a Minnesota courtroom.(2)

• Andrew Schindler, president of RJ Reynolds Tobacco, told a Florida lawyer in a deposition in 1997 that he doesn't think tobacco is any more addictive than coffee or carrots, and cited some obscure British research report done years ago on carrots.(3)

• During the same series of depositions Alexander Spears, chairman of Lorillard Tobacco Co., responded to the question on the number of Americans killed by cigarette smoking every year with this lesson in semantics: "It's an imponderable question. Nobody dies of cigarette smoking. You die of diseases." (4)

• "An excessive quantity of tomato juice would have done that, as I recall…" American Tobacco Co. CEO Donald Johnston, on August 19, 1997, when asked to comment on a 1953 research project where tobacco tars painted on the backs of mice produced tumors in 44% of the animals.(5)

• "It's unfair to the American public not to be honest." Steven Parrish, Senior Vice President, Philip Morris . August 14, 1995 (6)

• "Smoking kills. If you're killed, you've lost a very important part of your life." Brooke Shields, during an interview to become a spokesperson for a federal antismoking campaign. (7)

• "To cease smoking is the easiest thing I ever did; I ought to know because I have done it a thousand times." Mark Twain (8)

- "My mother gave up smoking when she was pregnant, but I don't think that would work with guys." (9)
- "Smoking is a dying habit." (10)

The Smoking Cardiologist's Recommendations

Q: I've heard that cardiovascular exercise can prolong life. Is this true?

A: Your heart is only good for so many beats, and that's it. Everything wears out eventually. Exercise will not make you live longer; that's like saying you can extend the life of your car by driving it faster. Might as well enjoy a rush of dopamine every hour or so, have a smoke and I wouldn't worry about it.

Q: Should I cut down on meat and eat more fruits and vegetables?

A: You must grasp logistical efficiencies. What does a cow eat? Hay and corn. And what are these? Vegetables. So, a steak is nothing more than an efficient mechanism of delivering vegetables to your system. Need organic matter? Smoke cigarettes. As many as possible.

Q: Is tobacco bad for me?

A: Look, it goes to the earlier point about fruits and vegetables. As we all know, scientists divide everything in the world into three categories: animal, mineral, and vegetable. We all know that tobacco is not animal, and it's a good idea to cut back on animal fat. My advice? Smoke as much as you want to. Just stay away from those high fat salad dressings.

Q: How can I calculate my body/fat ratio?

A: Well, if you have a body, and you have body fat, your ratio is one to one. If you have two bodies, your ratio is two to one, etc. That is called "statistically significant".

Q: At the gym, a guy asked me to "spot" for him while he did the bench press. What did he mean?

A: You're a smoker who goes to the gym? Why do you bother? It's an anti conspiracy to make you feel guilty. Anyway, "spotting" for someone means you stand over him while he blows air up your shorts. It's an accepted practice at health clubs; though if you find that it becomes the ONLY reason why you're going in, you probably ought to re-evaluate your exercise program. If he's a smoker, too, however, the air he blows up your shorts won't amount to much, so don't worry about it.

Q: What are some of the advantages of participating in a regular exercise program?

A: Can't think of a single one, sorry. My philosophy is: No Pain-No Pain. Have a smoke instead.

Q: If I stop smoking, will I live longer?

A: Nope. Smoking is a sign of individual expression and peace of mind. If you stop, you'll probably stress yourself to death in record time. So, you better smoke more. Two or three at a time is fine.

Q: Aren't fried foods bad for you?

A: You're not listening. Foods are fried these days in vegetable oil. In fact, they're permeated in it. How could getting more vegetables be bad for you? Some doctors classify tobacco as a vegetable. So, smoke a lot and you'll be fine.

Q: What's the secret to healthy eating?

A: After dinner cigars.

Q: Will sit-ups help prevent me from getting a little soft around the middle?

A: Definitely not! When you exercise a muscle, it gets bigger. You should only be doing sit-ups if you want a bigger stomach. Have a cigarette, instead. It's much better for you.

Top 10 News Headlines About Smoking and Cigarettes that You'll Never See (11)

10. New Study: Cigarette Smoke Makes Cars Smell Better
9. Movie Star's Secret for Looking Young: Chain Smoking
8. Cancer Cured! Smoking 5 Packs a Day Is the Answer
7. Tobacco Companies Decide to Stop Making Cigarettes for Health Reasons
6. Tobacco Executives Volunteer to Take Truth Serum
5. Proven Fact: A Pack A Day, Keeps the Doctor Away

4. Scientists Say Baby Formula Enhanced with Tobacco Makes Kids Smarter

3. Marlboro Man Dies of Lung Cancer — oh wait, I *did* see that headline!

2. School Distributes Cigarettes With Every Lunch. Parents Thrilled.

and the #1 news headlines about smoking and cigarettes that you'll never see...

1. Al Gore Invented Cigarettes (hmmm, maybe we WILL see that one)

Top 10 reasons Philip Morris finally admitted that cigarette smoking is addictive

10. Philip Morris admitted smoking is addictive to help the government to persuade addictive personalities to switch from pot and other illegal substances to a taxed drug that can be bought anywhere but church and school.

9. So people know there's a cheap alternative to heroin.

8. So smokers will stop trying to quit.

7. He said it when he was delirious from withdrawal. His lawyers wouldn't give him his cigarettes unless he confessed.

6. Philip Morris admitted that smoking is addictive in hopes of creating laughter in the administrative offices to prevent employees from wanting to sue them too.

5. It's all a big government conspiracy. They're trying to distract people's attention while the government relocates the martians that crashed at Roswell, New Mexico.

4. They changed their marketing campaign. They're now implementing the "truth in advertising" approach!

3. Luke Skywalker used a Jedi mind trick to get the executives to tell the truth.

2. April fools!

and the #1 reasons Philip Morris finally admitted that cigarette smoking is addictive...

1.   Hell just froze over.

RIDDLES!!!!

How do you manage to smoke ten cigarettes at once without looking like a circus act?
(Smoke a Cigar!!)

What do you call the industry who kills 400,000 of its most loyal customers every year?
(The tobacco industry)

How do you fit 4,000 chemicals into a space this size?
=====================================
(manufacture a cigarette)

What has twenty times the carcinogens of one cigarette?
(a package of cigarettes)

What do you call a skydiver who smokes?
(a cough drop)

~~~~~~~~~~~~~~~~~~~~~~~

All the cartoons are provided by the kind permission of, and credited to The Quit Smoking Company.

"I didn't think you'd mind me printing out a few tips on how to quit smoking off the Internet. There's only 871,926 of them."

"*I just thought I'd drop by personally and congratulate you on your accomplishment. No one has ever quit smoking 17,000 times in one year before.*"

"*You shall be arriving at the smoking section in a matter of minutes.*"

"You mean to tell me you climb 187 floors everyday to have a cigarette on the roof, and you claim you don't have a smoking problem?"

"What can I say? Ice cream makes me forget cigarettes."

"I know you're desperate, but that's not what I meant when I said to smoke the turkey."

"Go up and tell Jenkins that though I realize he's a little on edge from quitting smoking, he'll still have to pay for that computer."

• X - TOBACCO: PLAGUE OF THE NEW MILLENIUM •
Momentum Builds for a Smoke-Free World

"If current trends continue, tobacco will kill more than 100 million people in the first two decades of the 21st century." World Health Organization Fact Sheet 221, April 1999.

Where do we go from here?

California has set the pace for tobacco control, and the results to date offer encouragement for the future.

Since 1989, the per capita consumption of cigarettes has declined 52%. (1)

Between 1988 and 1996, lung and bronchus cancer rates in California have declined 14.4%, compared to the national rate of 4%. (2)

In 1988, 26.7% of California adults smoked; in 1998, 18.4% of adults smoked. (3)

Keep the cost of cigarettes high. In February, 1994 the Canadian federal government decreased tobacco taxes. Individual provinces received incentives to reduce provincial tobacco taxes. Following the reduction in tobacco taxes, the tobacco market increased by almost 10%, including a disturbing increase in youth smoking. (4)

Consumers have a choice: whether to invest the daily cost of smoking for their own use, or donate it to the tobacco industry. Young people who want to consider options other than setting their money on fire can be encouraged to examine the following information. The cost of smoking for a pack a day, starting at age 16, invested at a 10% annual rate translates into a monthly investment of $150. (5)

After 5 years (age 21) what would have been spent on cigarettes now totals 11,615.56

After 10 years (age 26) 30,726.74

After 15 years (age 31) 62,170.55

After 20 years (age 36) 113,905.32

After 25 years (age 41) 199,025.01

After 30 years (age 46) 339,072.19

After 35 years (age 51) 569,495.71

After 40 years (age 56) 948,611.94

A sixteen year old who chooses the option of investing the monthly cost of smoking and nothing else can retire at age 56 with a nest egg just under $1 million.

Sixteen year olds who smoke have chosen to donate their hard-earned after-tax dollars to the tobacco cartel receive blackened lungs, heart disease, cancer and emphysema at no extra cost. In B.C. where cigarettes cost $7.70 a pack, a sixteen year old can continue paying the salary of the industry working to entrap them, or put $7.70 aside each day until age 21 – and then be faced with the choice of how to spend $14,052.50.

"I bought'em [tobacco industry] an extra 20 – 30 years...But you know, it's temporary. One of these days we're going to have to pay up." David Hardy, on his deathbed, 1976, Chief outside tobacco attorney.

Tobacco's dirty secrets emerge like steam from a pressure cooker, sufficient to prevent one huge explosion and yet significant enough to attract attention. Now their attempts to hide information they have had and lied about for so long have become a matter of public record. The time has arrived to look at what to do with this information and use it as ammunition to address future tobacco efforts to draw on their previous success in duping governments, health authorities and the public.

European Parliament Approves Graphic Tobacco Packaging

In May, 2001, European Parliament approved tobacco packaging that would include graphic information about the health consequences of smoking, which will cover 33% of each cigarette package compared to the existing generic text which takes up 4% of each 'pack of fags'. The option is open whether or not to include the kind of photographs seen on Canadian cigarette packaging since January 2001. It also voted to outlaw the use of words such as *low* or *light* for cigarette advertising, and has introduced legislation to reduce tar levels from 12 mg. to l0 mg. per cigarette. (6)

Illustrating graphic effects of tobacco may have no more influence to stop anyone smoking than horrific photos of car crashes prevent anyone from driving. At least consumers who decide smoking must be part of their life can be in no doubt their choice also includes voluntarily inhaling the same lethal substance used in nazi gas chambers.

Other health warnings on Canadian cigarette packaging now in-

Smokers' Choice: The Same Gas Used in Nazi Gas Chambers, No Extra Cost

clude caution against smoking while pregnant and when around children, pathology photographs of a smokers' heart, lungs and brain – and a chilling reminder that in Canada, the equivalent of a small city dies every year from tobacco use.

How Does a Baby Get To Make An Adult Choice?

**"The days of glamorous cigarette packs
with obscure health warnings are over."
Catherine Stihler, U.K. Labour Health Spokesperson**

A Juror Speaks

Dr. Elizabeth Whelan is the founder and president of the American Council on Science and Health. Following the Boeken verdict in California in which Philip Morris were ordered to pay $5.8 billion to a Marlboro smoker with lung cancer, Dr. Whelan received the following letter from one of the jurors . (7)

"Dear Ms. Whelan:

Kudos for your article on the Boeken jury verdict. I was one of the jurors. You have done a pretty good job of divining our thinking.

Limbaugh and the others are nearly apoplectic on the subject of "individual responsibility." Well, that's something we discussed pretty thoroughly during our 8 days of deliberations. But we discussed another angle, as well—"Corporate Responsibility." And, while none of us were exactly fans of Mr. Boeken, we were pretty roundly shocked at Philip Morris' utter lack of responsibility to its customers over the past 50 years.

For me, it came down to a pretty simple mix: addictive drugs and kids. If you are deliberately getting kids addicted, then don't you DARE try to use "individual responsibility" as a defense.

I hope a lot more $ billion judgments follow. And I hope that Philip Morris soon follows Johns-Manville and spittoons on the road to extinction.
Best,
Peter Brosnan"

Tobacco Must Find Other Sources of Profit

Medical research, smoking bans, expensive punitive damages: these aspects of tobacco consumption raised red flags for tobacco business projections into the new millenium.

Tobacco knew diversification would be required to maintain profitable operation of business, and diversified into many areas, including food production. Philip Morris is Kraft Foods, for example, and R. J. R. Nabisco is R. J. Reynolds Tobacco. A detailed list and references for further research appear in the following pages of tobacco-owned non-tobacco interests. It remains for individuals to decide whether choices should include supporting an industry who, for roughly a century, diligently deceived health authorities and the public, by secretly manipulating levels of addictive substances in their products, for as long as they could get away with doing so. For at least half a century they managed to maintain this scam, with devastating consequences. How do consumers know the same tactics will not be used to taint food to ensure customers return for more?

"The stakes in this ongoing public relations battle are enormous. On one side of the ledger is the health of more than 200 million

teen-agers and adults. One (sic) the other side are [the] profits, even survival, of the tobacco industry in dependence on the 55.8 million addicted smokers as of 1988." Health and Morality – Tobacco's Counter Campaign, 1992, Bates No. 2022849007/9028

The health benefits of quitting smoking end this book on a positive note. From a twelve step program through Nicotine Anonymous (8) to smoking cessation clinics arranged through medical authorities, overcoming nicotine addiction becomes a reality for thousands of smokers each year.

What difference does it make to quit smoking?
Within 20 minutes of smoking that last cigarette, the body begins a series of changes that continues for years (9)

20 Minutes following a cigarette
- Blood pressure drops to normal
- Pulse rate drops to normal
- Body temperature of hands and feet increases to normal

8 Hours
- Carbon monoxide level in blood drops to normal
- Oxygen level in blood increases to normal

24 Hours
- Chance of heart attack decreases

48 Hours
- Nerve endings start regrowing
- Ability to smell and taste is enhanced

2 Weeks to Three Months
- Circulation improves
- Walking becomes easier
- Lung function increases up to 30%

1 – 9 Months
- Coughing, sinus congestion, fatigue, and shortness of breath decrease

- Cilia regrow in lungs, increasing ability to handle mucus, clean the lungs, and reduce infection
- Body's overall energy increases

1 Year
- Excess risk of coronary heart disease is half that of a smoker

5 Years
- Lung cancer death rate for average smoker (one pack a day) decreases by almost half
- Stroke risk is reduced to that of a nonsmoker 5-15 years after quitting
- Risk of cancer of the mouth, throat and esophagus is half that of a smoker's

10 Years
- Lung cancer death rate similar to that of nonsmokers
- Precancerous cells are replaced
- Risk of cancer of the mouth, throat, esophagus, bladder, kidney and pancreas decreases

15 Years
- Risk of coronary heart disease is that of a nonsmoker

Summary

To any teenager who might be considering whether to experiment with tobacco, give some thought to whether your decision includes wanting to experiment with drug addiction.

As teenagers reach the age of consent, freedom to make their own choices awaits them. A tobacco choice ensures dependency upon nicotine and return for repeat business, guaranteeing tobacco maintains its multi-billion dollar profits each year. The alternative choice can be to invest the price of a daily package of cigarettes from the age of sixteen and decide how to spend just under $15,0000 on their 21st birthday. When investment of the price of a pack of cigarettes a day is taken as seriously as smoking, the same 16 year old who chooses smoke-free can realize investment capital of $948,611.94 by the age of 56.

By the age of 56, the l6-year old who chose smoke-free and invested carefully can expect financial freedom and the guarantee that one avoidable health risk has been eliminated. By the age of 56, many smokers have already experienced their first (and possibly second) heart attack, stroke and/or diagnosis of lung cancer and/or emphysema. Their hard-earned after-tax dollars have, literally, gone up in smoke and left in their wake charred lungs, an overworked heart and malfunctioning circulatory system.

A new type of smoking sign has already made its appearance. The future is now.

Sign of the Times from Our Friends in Lubbock, Texas

The internet facilitates delivery into private homes of material found in some of the best reference libraries in the world.

Available information about the tobacco industry grows each day, as tobacco truths replace the decades of lies, fraud and cover-ups.

Those addicted to nicotine who want to stop smoking often become discouraged after unsuccessful attempts and often are ashamed to admit publicly just how hooked they have become on nicotine. Online resources have helped thousands to find camaraderie and emotional support, working hand in glove with medically supervised cessation programs. The need of anonymity for many need not hamper successful attempts to overcome nicotine addiction. Permanently.

Scientists and doctors have worked for many years researching and confirming the devastation caused by tobacco. Information once available only to professionals has become available to anyone who knows where to look, in a format easily understood by the non-scientists and non-doctors among us.

Those who have chosen a smoke-free life have united against what has until recent years been a smokers' world that normalizes nicotine addiction.

No substitute exists for real libraries and real books. The following internet sites can be considered a springboard for further reading.

Smoking Cessation

1. Nicotine Anonymous, based on a twelve-step programme to overcome substance addiction http://www.nicotine-anonymous.org/
2. The Quit Smoking Company, an excellent and varied support site with practical information, also the source of the cartoons and Top Ten Lists in Chapter IX *Cigarette Lighter Side: Mouth Fires and Comical Tobacco Liars* http://www.quitsmoking.com/
3. Physicians for a Smoke-Free Canada smoking cessation links http://www.smoke-free.ca/Health/pschealth_quitting.htm
4. American Academy of Family Physicans, Smoking Cessation in Recovering Alcoholics http://familydoctor.org/handouts/269.html
5. Medline Plus Health Information: Smoking Cessation http://www.nlm.nih.gov/medlineplus/smokingcessation.html
6. British Columbia, Canada Doctors' Stop Smoking Program http://www.bcdssp.com/
7. The Nicstick A product invented and manufactured in B.C. has helped many http://web43.radiant.net/~nicstick/

Adolescents and Tobacco

1. Dr. Jeffrey Wigand founded this non-profit organization to educate students about tobacco. An excellent resource site with contacts for questions about tobacco and the organization's activities. http://www.jeffreywigand.com/insider/sfk.html
2. British Columbia, Canada Ministry of Health: Youth Tobacco Attack Team. The Tobacco Child and Sucked In posters available. Puke page, educators' resource material available by mailorder http://www.tobaccofacts.org/
3. Kick the Nic: Youth Smoking Cessation online support and information http://www.tobaccofacts.org/smoker1-kicknic.html

4.   S.W.A.T. (Students Working Against Tobacco) excellent site for infor-
      mation, peer support, sponsored activities http://www.wholetruth.com/

Smoke-Free Rights Support

1.   Clean Air Coalition, Vancouver, B.C.
      http://www.cleanaircoalitionbc.com/
2.   AIRSPACE Action on Smoking and Health, Vancouver, B.C.
      www.airspace.bc.ca
3.   ASH Action on Smoking and Health. Custody battles, current
      events, updated medical research: all tobacco-related. http://ash.org/
4.   Nonsmokers' Rights Association: Canadian Smoking and Health
      Action Foundation. Also in French.
      http://www.nsra-adnf.ca/english/index.html
5.   Americans for Nonsmokers' Rights: Helplines, current news, hot
      documents http://www.no-smoke.org/
6.   Smoke Free Action Network. Joe Cherner site
      http://www.smokefreeair.org/
7.   Smoke-Free World. International listing for the smoke free travel-
      ler http://www.smokefreeworld.com

**"Opportunity exists for a cigarette manufacturer to dominate...high
incidents (sic) of smoking and drugs in subcultures."** *Project SCUM*
R.J. Reynolds Tobacco December 12, 1995 Bates 51802-1124

• EPILOGUE •

The unconditional support, encouragement and practical help from my husband has assisted me beyond words to see this project to completion. His perplexity over the hours I have spent poring over articles in medical journals (and talking to doctors all over the world who wrote them), legal documents and other tobacco-related information has been replaced by a shared rage about tobacco wool pulled over everyone's eyes for so long.

In closing, his comments:

Now tobacco deception has been revealed in their own words, we are left to ponder what manner of people would knowingly manufacture and market a product that dependably addicts, sickens, maims, and kills. There seems to have been extensive collusion with governments at all levels, the judiciary system and even Hollywood. Big tobacco has successfully managed surreptitiously to bribe, threaten, and otherwise coerce those able to sustain tobacco's status quo, also to subvert and re-direct the irrefutable medical evidence about consequences of tobacco use. The industry has been allowed to continue selling a lethal product virtually unimpeded.

Not only tobacco growers, but manufacturers, distributors, advertisers, sellers and even the corner grocery store accept blood money every time a ten year old purchases candy flavored snuff, every time a twelve year old buys a pack of cigarettes, every time a pipe smoker purchases a coumarin-laced refill, and any time they sell tobacco products to anybody. Purveyors of tobacco comply with the accepted definition of drug dealers, who justify profit with the rationalization if they didn't sell the product, someone else would. Tobacco addicts as heroin does, yet legalization of heroin is fiercely resisted. Tobacco, whose consumption kills more every year than heroin, AIDS, suicides, alcohol abuse and car accidents – combined – has legions of apologists who ignore the truth and reassure each other with self-serving falsehoods that tobacco is "no worse" than getting a tan, drinking coffee or driving a car.

For the young, modern life is fraught with dangers and regrettable decisions, not least of which is whether to experiment with tobacco. You have been handed, and many of you have accepted, the misleading concept that smoking is "adult" and "cool" and "rebellious". Big tobacco love you for it, and encourage you to consider yourself a "free thinker", each time original thought is forfeited when you copy what you see others doing. Each time you accept a light because your free thinking does not want you to be different from those currently in your company, you allow nicotine to maintain a foothold in your decision-making process and any prospect of free thinking goes up in smoke.

After only three cigarettes, your brain chemistry alters sufficiently to begin a chemical dependence on regular nicotine fixes if the unpleasant symptoms of withdrawal are to be avoided. With each puff of that next cigarette, your brain receives its dose of nicotine and the anxious irritable, intolerant, angry feelings are replaced by pleasure and relief – similar to the heroin addict shooting up, although the heroin addict must wait twice as long as a smoker for his drug of choice to affect brain chemistry. To believe otherwise ignores what addiction experts around the world now know without doubt, and clearly illustrates the denial typically accompanying any kind of drug dependency.

Amos Hausner, a Jerusalem attorney, has suggested all tobacco executives be brought before an international tribunal and charged with crimes against humanity. Considering the millions tobacco has killed, this suggestion certainly has merit.

The tobacco industry likes to use the word "choice" when referring to the use of its products. Their mantra has been smoking is a "choice" and once adult status has been achieved, "freedom to choose" becomes a constitutional right – as long as you choose to smoke, of course. Tobacco never addresses the constitutional rights of the smoke free to remain that way. Tobacco never suggest to a young person considering smoking they visit a palliative care ward to ask the smoker dying in agony from cancer about "choice".

Tobacco never tell you that addiction *removes* choices. C.W.L.

Tobacco's Non-Tobacco Interests

Tobacco tentacles reach far, and extend into every aspect of industry and commerce. Today's consumers can choose to move forward by boycotting goods and services that contribute to profits of the tobacco cartel. For every consumer item or service listed, alternative choices exist. (1)

Philip Morris' Non-Tobacco Companies and Brands:

Miller Genuine Draft	Lowenbrau
Miller Lite	Red Dog
Miller High Life	Milwaukee's Best

Kraft Foods Brands (wholly owned by Philip Morris):

DAIRY:

Kraft Macaroni Cheese	Minute Tapioca
Velveeta cheese product	Athenos Cheese
Philadelphia Cream Cheese	Cheez Whiz
Knudsens	Cracker Barrel
Breyers	Sealtest
Kraft Parmesan	Breakstone's
Kraft Singles	Light N Lively
Kraft Taste of Life	

POST Cereals:

Alpha-Bits	Banana Nut Crunch
Grape Nuts	Pebbles
Raisin Bran	Toasties

RJR NABISCO (R.J. Reynolds Tobacco):

Oreo Cookies	Air Crisps
Chips Ahoy!	Wheat Thins,
Snackwell's	Nilla, Nutter Butter
Newtons	Stella D'Oro
Ritz Crackers	Better Cheddars
Premium Saltines	Cheese Nips
Nabisco Honey Maid Grahams	Toastettes
Triscuit	Barnum's Animal Crackers

LIFESAVERS:

Life Savers	Bubble Yum
Breath Savers	Gummi Savers
Care*Free	Ice Breakers

MISCELLANEOUS:

Minute Rice	Cool Whip
Miracle Whip	Dream Whip
Jell-O	Claussen Pickles
Good Seasons	DiGiorno Italian Sauces
Sure Jell	Calumet Baking Powder
Certo	Shake 'N Bake
Kool-Aid	Oven Fry
Seven Seas	Altoids
Country Time	Toblerone Chocolate
Taco Bell Home Originals	Stove Top Stuffing

Baker's Chocolate and other Baking Products

Maxwell House Coffee	Stove Top Stuffing
Sanka	Capri Juice Drinks
Yuban Coffee	Crystal Light

General Foods International Coffee

Tang Bull's Eye Barbecue Sauce

DELI:
Oscar Meyer Products
Louis Rich Products

PLANTERS NUTS etc.:

Roasted Peanuts, Cashews

Manufactures and markets sauces and condiments, pet snacks, hot cereals, dry mix desserts and gelatins that include such brand names as A1, Grey Poupon, Milk-Bone, Cream of Wheat, Royal and Knox.

Full information on tobacco-owned subsidiaries and office addresses appears on the website of Conscientious ConsumingTM http://www.conscientiousconsuming.com/Tobacco/Boycott_Tobacco.htm

• NOTES •
DEDICATION

(1)   *Weird Business Rides Again: Houston Chronicle*, Jim Barlow July
        23, 1997
(2)   *Jurors in Smokers' Trial Will see Anti-Smoking Video: Polk Online:
        Associated Press* November 3, 1998

GENESIS
A CHRONOLOGY OF THE MARKETING OF NICOTINE
ADDICTION

(1)   King James I *Counterblaste to Tobacco*, 1604
(2)   Harvard Center for Cancer Prevention, Lung Cancer Fact Sheet
(3)   *History of Advertising Archives* , August 1987 by Richard Pollay,
        Curator, Professor of Marketing, University of British Columbia
        Faculty of Commerce Bates No. 2024985261/5290
(4)   *A Frank Statement to Cigarette Smokers* January 4, 1954, Philip
        Morris Bates Number 2015002376
(5)   *Ibid*
(6)   *Ibid*
(7)   *History of Advertising Archives,* August 1987 by Richard Pollay,
        Curator, Professor of Marketing, University of British Columbia Fac-
        ulty of Commerce. Page 24 Bates Number 2024985261/5290
(8)   *Report of the Scientific Committee on Tobacco and Health: Effect of
        Tobacco Advertising on Tobacco Consumption: A discussion docu-
        ment reviewing the evidence.* C. Smee, M. Parsonage, R. Anderson,
        S. Duckworth, 1992. London: Economics & Operational Research
        Division, Dept. of Health
(9)   *Tobacco Advertising* Dutch Foundation on Smoking and Health. Marc
        C. Willemsen & Boudewijn de Blij
(10)   *Ibid* (8)
(11)   *Ibid*
(12)   *Ibid*
(13)   *The New York Times Bans All Tobacco Advertising in Publications:
        The Digital Collegian* April 30, 1999
(14)   WCB To Introduce Amendments to Environmental Tobacco Smoke
        Regulations Press Release, March 8, 2001

I - WOMEN AND CHILDREN FIRST
Tobacco Targets the Vulnerable

(1) *Project Magic* December 1985 Philip Morris "qualitative research" document Bates number 2501008130/8154

(2) *A Flapper's Appeal to Parents* by Ellen Welles Page, Outlook Magazine December 6, 1922

(3) *"Smoking initiation by adolescent girls, 1944 through 1988: An association with targeted advertising,"* Journal of the American Medical Association 1994, Vol. 271, No. 8 Pierce J.P., Lee L., Gilpin E.A.,

(4) CDC, *"Youth Risk Behavior Surveillance – United States, 1999,"* *MMWR*, 9 June 2000, Vol. 49, No. SS-5

(5) Harvard Centre for Cancer Prevention Fact Sheet

(6) *Counter Campaign Launched Against Virginia Slims "Find Your Voice" Ads Targeted Toward Women:* National Clearinghouse for Alcohol and Drug Information: *NCADI Reporter,* May 30, 2000

(7) *Ibid*

(8) Washington U.S. Newswire June 27, 2001 *Campaign for Tobacco-Free Kids Background Info on Women, Girls and Tobacco*

(9) *Ibid* (1)

(10) *Ibid*

(11) ABC News: *Women and Cigarettes, The Fatal Attraction*, Dr. Nancy Snyderman, July 5, 2001

(12) Philip Morris Special Report – *Young Smokers: Prevalence, Trends, Implications and Related Demographic Trends.* March 31, 1981. Bates No. 1000390808 & 1000290810

(13) February 29, 1984 RJR document, *"Young Adult Smokers: Strategies and Opportunities* Bates No. 5024-11168-70-77

(14) *Protecting B.C. Kids from Tobacco*, British Columbia Ministry of Health, Tobacco Facts

(15) *Ibid*

(16) *Cherry Chew: Tobacco for Tots. Communication Works*

(17) *Federal Register* August 11, 1995 page 41331

(18) *Sales-Marketing Magazine* . In-house publication for R.J.Reynolds Tobacco Bates No. 509717145, 509718148

(19) *RJR Nabisco's Cartoon Camel Promotes Camel Cigarettes to Children.* DiFranza, JR. Richards JW. et al. Journal of the American Medical Association. 1991: 266: 3149-3153. Bates No. 515011357/362

(20) *Brand logo recognition by 3- to 6-year-old children*: Fischer PM, Schwartz MP, Richards JW Jr, Goldstein AO, Rojas TH Mickey Mouse and Old Joe the Camel. Journal of the American Medical Association 1991: 266: 3145-3148.

(21)   James Johnston, CEO of R.J. Reynolds Tobacco, in testimony
        before the House Energy and Commerce Subcommittee on Health
        and the Environment, April 14, 1994. Tobacco Control Archives:
        Mangini Collection. R. J. Reynolds document Number 939359
(22)   March 15, 1976, document stamped "secret" and entitled *Planning
        Assumptions and Forecast for the period 1977-1986 for R.J.
        Reynolds Tobacco* Bates Number 500774787 *page* 14
(23)   *R J Reynolds Targets 14 Year Olds:* James Johnston, CEO of R.J.
        Reynolds Tobacco, in testimony before the House Energy and Com-
        merce Subcommittee on Health and the Environment, April 14, 1994.
        Dept. of Public Health and Community Medicine. University of Sydney.
(24)   *Ibid*
(25)   R.J. Reynolds 1994 Advertising Campaign: Public Citizen *"Don't Be
        Fooled Again"*, American Lung Association
(26)   Claude Teague of R.J. Reynolds Tobacco in his *"Research Plan-
        ning Memorandum on Some Thoughts About New Brands of
        Cigarettes for the Youth Market,"* February 2, 1973. Bates No.
        502987358
(27)   *Ibid* (25)   Geoffrey Bible CEO of Philip Morris testifying and
        responding to a question at Minnesota tobacco trial in St. Paul,
        February 1998.
(28)   *Ibid* 1979 Philip Morris internal memorandum
(29)   *Ibid* 1994 Tobacco Industry Advertisement
(30)   *Apparently Problematic Research,* a Brown & Williamson Tobacco
        document which Judge Fitzpatrick ruled was placed in an advertising
        category, instead of one relating to minors, *Minneapolis -St. Paul
        Star Tribune* March 8, 1998
(31)   Philip Morris Vice-President for Research and Development *Why
        One Smokes*, first draft, Autumn 1969 Minnesota Trial Exhibit 3681
(32)   R. J. Reynolds, Summary of Decisions Made in MRD-ESTY
        Meeting April 7, 1971 Minnesota Trial Exhibit 12,258
(33)   *Share of Smokers by Age Group,* T. Key. August 12, 1976. Minne-
        sota Trial, Exhibit 12,238
(34)   *Ibid* (32) Philip Morris Memo, 1979. Minnesota Attorney General
(35)   Philip Morris Marketing Research Document *Incidence of Smoking
        Cigarettes* May 18, 1973. Minnesota Trial Exhibit 11,801
(36)   *An Adman's Confession: Medical Journal of Australia,* March 5,
        1983 page 237
(37)   Martha Groves, *"Tobacco Firm's Gift Viewed as a Marketing
        Smoke Screen." Los Angeles Times*, November 29, 2000
(38)   *Some Thoughts About How To get FUBYAS (Marlboro Smokers)
        To Switch* R.J. Reynolds Tobacco Company.. Bates Number
        504656759/65

(39)   *"Less Educated Smoker" Overview of the Market's Education Level*:
        R. J. Reynolds Tobacco Company. Bates Number 50753 4569

(40)   *Ibid   Bates Number 50753 4570*

(41)   Letter to R. J. Reynolds from McCann-Erickson on the "Less Edu-
        cated Smoker" Bates Number 50461 7417

(42)   *Project SCUM,* R.J. Reynolds Tobacco December 12, 1995 . Bates
        Number 518021121 – 518021122

(43)   *Topline Report on Eight Focus Groups with Women Smokers About
        Issues Related to new Virginia Slims Kings.* December 1991. Bates
        2057763894/3911

(44)   April 8, 1982 Philip Morris Inter-office memorandum from T.S. Osdene
        to Hugh Cullman *"Biological Effects of Smokeless Tobacco Products"*

(45)   *Science News,* Cornell University. *Cornell University Child Abuse
        Expert Says It's Time to Recognize Smoking as Child Abuse* Septem-
        ber 26, 1997

II - THEY WILL GO DOWN IN HISTORY
Tobacco Saints & Ain'ts

(1)   JAMA Editorial July 19, 1995 *The Brown and Williamson Docu-
        ments – Where Do We Go From Here?* Vol. 273 #3 pages 199-202

(2)   Vermilion 1999, ISBN 0 09 181665 3, 256 pages

(3)   Tobacco Enforcement Section, Office of Attorney General, Harris-
        burg Pennsylvania *"Targeting of African Americans"*

(4)   Center for Communications, Health and the Environment (CECHE)
        *"Truly Retiring the Marlboro Man"; Extending U.S. Marketing
        and Labelling Restrictions Abroad.* May 26, 2000

(5)   Repace & Associates Inc. *"Factsheet on Secondhand Smoke"*
        September 1, 1999

(6)   U.S. Department of Health and Human Services, National Toxicol-
        ogy Program, Pursuant to Section 301 (b) (4) of the Public Health
        Service Act as Amended by Section 262, PL95-622 *9th Report on
        Carcinogens* Revised January 2001

(7)   *Dilemma for Journals Over Tobacco Cash: Nature* magazine, Au-
        gust 13, 1998

(8)   *Ibid*

(9)   *Ibid*

(10)   The Augusta Chronicle: *Scientists Claim Secondhand Smoke, Alco-
        hol, Carcinogens,* Dec. 4, 1998

(11)   *Cigarette Papers: Lawyer Management of Scientific Research
        Stanton A. Glantz, John Slade, Lisa A. Bero, Peter Hanauer,
        Deborah E.Barnes. Chapter 8, part 3, table 8.1 "CTR Special
        Products Awarded to Theodor Sterling" page 5*

(12)   *Ibid*
(13)   *"Dilemma of a Cigarette Exporter" The Guardian,* February 3, 2000, Kenneth Clarke
(14)   *The Sunday Times "Clarke in Row Over Tobacco Company Deal,* June 24, 2001
(15)   *British Medical Journal Survey,* May, 2001
(16)   ASH letter to Sir Colin Campbell December 8, 2000
(17)   *The Times of London,* June 12, 2001 *"University Cancer Team Quits Over Tobacco Aid"*
(18)   *Ibid*
(19)   *Montreal Gazette,* June 21, 2001
(20)   *Ibid*
(21)   document ID 2406.03, Brown & Williamson Collection
(22)   Expanded formal petition, complaint and request for a formal criminal investigation of hidden cigarette ads in movies intended for theatres and therefore in violation of 15 U.S.C. 1333 and hidden cigarette ads in movies intended for television and therefore in violation of 15 U.S.C. 1335, May 12, 1998, by Action on Smoking and Health.

III - TOBACCO BRAND OF SCIENCE
Hire Scientists Who Will Make It So

(1)   *Ibid Chapter I (4)*
(2)   *British Medical Journal,* August 5, 2000, *"Operation Berkshire": the international tobacco companies' conspiracy"* (Education and Debate) Author/s: Neil Francey, Barrister at Law, Sydney, Australia; Simon Chapman, Associate Professor, Dept. of Public Health & Community Medicine, University of Sydney, Australia
(3)   Letter, March 24, 1977, from R.A. Garrett, CEO Imperial Tobacco to Alexander Holtzman, Associate General Counsel for Philip Morris Bates Number 2025025341/5343
(4)   Position Paper, April 28, 1977 Bates Number 2501024572/4575
(5)   *Ibid*
(6)   *Ibid*
(7)   *Ibid*
(8)   Letter August 12, 1977 Bates Number 1003727234/7235
(9)   Letter June 28, 1977 Bates Number 2501024528
(10)   *Pioneer Planet: Ex-tobacco researcher cites Fifth over industry records.* Thomas J. Collins, Staff Writer. February 18,
(11)   *Ibid (2)*
(12)   Chelsea Group Limited *Our People*
(13)   Agreement October 20, 1993 , Bates No.2024207277

(14)   August 12, 1994 *Comments on OSHA Proposed IAQ Rule* Philip Morris Bates 2057835001

(15)   *Ventilation Issues Update* GASP of Colorado Education Library. January 2000.

(16)   June 12, 1996 National Smokers Alliance letter from Member Services

(17)   *Los Angeles Times: Tobacco Institute Workers Confident of Reincarnation*, Marlene Cimons June 24, 1997

(18)   British Columbia Ministry of Health: *Tobacco Facts: Tobacco Timeline 1997 – 2001*

(19)   *Los Angeles Times: Smoker Group's Thick Wallet Raises Questions* Myron Levin

(20)   *"Whitecoat"* memo Bates 2023542534A November 16, 1987

(21)   Notes on a Special Meeting of the U.K. Industry on Environmental Tobacco Smoke February 17, 1988 Bates 2063791181/1187

(22)   *Ibid*

(23)   *Ibid*

(24)   *Ibid*

(25)   *Man Identifies Tobacco Firm's Paid Stooge at Lancet: The Guardian* May 16, 1998, Clare Dyer

(26)   David Hanners, *Scientists paid to write on tobacco Letters aimed to discredit report on secondhand smoke's effects.* SAINT PAUL PIONEER PRESS, August 14, 1998

(27)   *Ibid*

(28)   *Ibid*

(29)   *Ibid*

(30)   Tobacco Industry Documents in the Minnesota Depository: Implications for Global Tobacco Control. *Briefing Paper No. 3 (February 1999) : Industry Recruitment of Scientific Experts,* Norbert Hirschhorn, M.D.

(31)   *Ibid*

(32)   *Controlling Globally, Acting Locally: Multinational Tobacco Companies and Legislation to Protect Workers and the Public from Secondhand Smoke* Physicians for a Smoke-Free Canada Submission to the Workers' Compensation Board of British Columbia , June 2000, page 2

(33)   *Ibid*

(34)   INFACT REPORT: *Pulling Out All the Stops: Philip Morris Fight to Block FDA Regulation of Tobacco* March 21, 2000

(35)   FORCES Independent Research Profile: Rosalind Marimont

(36)   Cato Institute: Policy Staff Robert A. Levy profile

(37)   *Ibid* (26)

(38)   *Ibid* Chapter II (19)

(39)   Philip Morris Press Release September 28, 1993 Bates No. 2060579242

(40)   Norfolk Genetic Information Network *Big Tobacco Behind Euro Anti-Organic Campaign* November 28, 2000
(41)   APCO Associates Inc Memorandum to M. Winokur from T. Hockaday, N. Cohen: "Thoughts on TASSC Europe" March 25, 1994 Bates Number 2025492898/2905
(42)   *PR WATCH: How Big Tobacco Helped Create "the Junkman"*, Sheldon Rampton and John Stauber, Volume 7, No. 3, p. 9
(43)   *Ibid* (32) pp 14-15
(44)   *Ibid*
(45)   *EXTRA!: The Ascendancy of Conrad Black* Barbara Leiterman November/December/1996
(46)   *Campus Life University of Toronto: Corporate Rules on Campus*, Brian Sharpe Fall 1998
(47)   *Ibid* (43)
(48)   World Health Organization Press Release WHO/29: *PASSIVE SMOKING DOES CAUSE LUNG CANCER, DO NOT LET THEM FOOL YOU* March 9, 1998
(49)   *Market Guide: Philip Morris Companies: Murdoch, Rupert*
(50)   Institute for Public Accuracy *Cato Institute: Libertarian in a Corporate Way*, Robert Solomon December 1997
(51)   *Geoffrey C. Bible, CEO of Philip Morris Co.s Inc. Voted onto News Corp.'s Board June 23: Richmond-times Dispatch* C. Jones
(52)   *Leading Families: Your Teenager and Smoking: Understanding the Issue and Preventing the Habit Factsheet: Myth Three: Exercise Counteracts the Effects of Smoking* Knowledge Gain Publications6
(53)   *CBS News 60 Minutes II: The Low Tar Myth* February 20, 2001
(54)   "Resistance to Draw Depends on Flow Rate and Cigaret Construction" Bates Number0000260491
(55)   *Ibid* (53)
(56)   *Ibid* (54)
(57)   Chart 5: Comparison Table for tar delivery of Winston cigarets [sic] Bates Number 0000260476
(58)   *The Digital Collegian Pennsylvania State University: Vent Holes Key to Healthier Light Cigarettes* January 19, 1995, Amy Oakes
(59)   L.F. Meyer inter-office memorandum to B. Goodman, Philip Morris U.S.A. September 17, 1975 . Minnesota Trial Exhibit 11,564 Bates Number 202154488
(60)   *Journal of the American Medical Association: A "Safer" Cigarette? Prove It, Say Critics* Joan Stephenson, Ph.D. Vol. 283, No. 19, May 17, 2000
(61)   *FORUM Environmental Health Perspectives:Help Stopping Smoking* Volume 107, Number 4, April 1999

(62) *Lung Association Calls for Withdrawal of Eclipse Nicotine Delivery Device from Market* American Lung Association Statement of John R. Garrison, CEO April 20, 2000

(63) Canadian Cancer Society: Smoking and Health: Fifty Most Often Asked Questions about Smoking and Health. [36]

(64) *Ibid*

(65) *Root Technology: A Handbook for Leaf Blenders and Product Developers* British American Tobacco Co. Bates Number 401095572

(66) "Project Coumarin – Top Secret" Philip Morris Oslo internal memorandum March 10, 1987 Dates Number 2501046314

(67) *Ibid*

(68) National Toxicology Program : Coumarin: Identifiers, Carcinogenity

(69) *FORUM Environmental Health Perspectives Volume 102, Number 9 : They Put THAT in Cigarettes?* Volume 102, Number 9, September 1994 page 7

(70) *History of Advertising Archives,* Richard Pollay, Curator, Professor of Marketing, Faculty of Commerce, University of British Columbia: *Chronological Notes on the History of Cigarette Advertising* August 1987 page 18 Bates 2024985281

(71) Foundation for National Progress: Mojo Wire: *Mother Jones JA93: Heavy Breathing – The Maker of Kents withheld information about its deadly asbestos filter* L.J. Davis

(72) *Ibid*

(73) *Selected Advertising Text Messages United States, 1929-2000* National Academies Office of News and Public Information, National Research Council; 1952 Kent Cigarette Advertisement

(74) *Selected Verdicts: 2000: Jury Awards $1,048,100.00 in Kent Micronite Asbestos Cigarette Filter Case* Brayton & Purcell (plaintiff's attorney), Novato, California

(75) *Mistaken Ruling, Unmistakable Facts: How Judge Osteen Got It Wrong When He Vacated the EPA's Finding that Secondhand Smoke is a Known Carcinogen* , Graham Kelder, Managing Attorney, Northeastern University of Law, Boston, Massachusetts page 5

(76) *Ibid* page 6

(77) *Ibid* page 1

(78) Press Release September 15, 1998: United States Environmental Protection Agency, Washington, Office of Communications, Education and Public Affairs

IV - TOBACCO BRAND OF SILENCE
Why Tell The Truth When Lies Sound Better?

(1)   Tobacco Abroad: *Infiltrating Foreign Markets*, David Holzman
         FOCUS Volume 105, No. 102. February 1997, page 1

(2)   *Ibid* page 1
(3)   *Ibid* page 4
(4)   *Ibid* page 2
(5)   *Ibid* page 3
(6)   *Revealed: Clarke's Link to $40m Vietnam Tobacco Deal, The
         Observer*, Antony Barnett, Public Affairs Editor. June 24, 2001
(7)   *Ibid* (1) page 4
(8)   International Union Against Cancer Factsheet 11: *Youth and Tobacco*
(9)   *Truly Retiring the Marlboro Man: Extending U.S. Marketing and
         Labeling Restrictions Abroad.* CECHE
(10)   *Joe Camel Goes to Europe: Washington Post* April 2, 1998
(11)   *Ibid*
(12)   *Ibid*
(13)   Federal Trade Commission Report to Congress pursuant to the
         Federal Cigarette Labeling & Advertising Act, issued July 28, 1999
(14)   ASH Action on Smoking and Health Press Release: *New Docu-
         ments Prove Tobacco Industry Planted Hidden Ads in Kids'
         Movies: Justice Department Asked to Indict Since Movies Failed
         to Carry Warning.* May 12, 1998
(15)   Tobacco Enforcement Section, Office of the Attorney General:
         *Industry Control and Manipulation of Nicotine to Foster Addiction
         and Thus Profits* C: Suppression and Concealment of Research on
         Nicotine Addiction 179
(16)   *Ibid* 180
(17)   63-page pretrial sworn deposition of Dr. Jeffrey Wigand. Novem-
         ber 29, 1995. Pp 43-44
(18)   *Ibid* (15) 184
(19)   *Ibid*   185
(20)   *Ibid* 186
(21)   Tobacco Free Initiative: Health Impact World Health Organization

V - SECONDHAND SMOKE, FIRSTHAND POLLUTION
Tiny Smokestacks Poison a Room

(1)   *Periodic Survey of Fellows,* American Academy of Pediatrics,
         Division of Health Policy Research
(2)   *Passive Smoking and Heart Disease: Epidemiology, Physiology*

and Biochemistry, S. A. Glantz and W. W. Parmley. Circulation 83: 1-2, 1991

(3)   *Smoking Sparks Controversy: Amarillo Business* Journal Dr. Roby Mitchell January 6, 1997

(4)   *Tobacco Kills – Don't Be Duped* American Association for World Health May 31, 2000

(5)   *Dietary Nicotine: Won't Mislead on Passive Smoking* J.L. Repace, M.Sc., M. Jarvis, M.D., University College London Dept. Epidemiology & Public Health *British Medical Journal* January 1994 308:61 62

(6)   *Cornell University Science News,* Gabarino, James. September 26, 1997

(7)   *Passive Smoking: Children Don't Have A Choice!* Jan Anderson, We Women U.K. August 5, 2001

(8)   *Involuntary Smoking – A Hazard to Children:* Committee on Environmental Hazards, American Academy of Pediatrics, *Pediatrics* Vol 77, 1986, reconfirmed 1991

(9)   *Effect of Maternal Cigarette Smoking on Pregnancy Complications and Sudden Infant Death Syndrome,* Joseph DiFranza and Robert Lew, *Journal of Family Practice* 1995; 40: 385-394

(10)   *Involuntary Smoking – A Hazard to Children;* Committee on Environmental Hazards, American Academy of Pediatricians, *Pediatrics* Vol 77, 1986, reconfirmed 1991

(11)   *Morbidity and Mortality in Children Associated with the Use of Tobacco Products by Other People,* Joesph De Franza and Robert Lew, *Pediatrics 1995; 97: 560-568*

(12)   *Ibid*

(13)   *Ibid*

(14)   *Ibid*

(15)   *10 Steps to Keep the Children in Your Practice Nonsmokers.* Roger Thomas, M.D., Ph.D., University of Ottawa, Ontario *American Family Physician, Volume 54, No. 2,* August 1996

(16)   *American Academy of Pediatrics Child Health Month: Things You Should Know About* ETS October 1997: Risk *Management of Passive Smoking at Work and at Home.* James Repace, M.Sc.

(17)   Action on Smoking and Health: *Custody & Smoking: Digest of Important Legal Developments Related to Custody and Smoking* pp 4 - 6

(18)   *Ibid* p 6

(19)   *Ibid*

(20)   *Ibid*

(21)   *Ibid* pp 6-7

(22)   *Ibid* p 7

(23)   *Ibid*

(24)   *Ibid*

(25)   *Ibid*
(26)   *Ibid*
(27)   *Ibid*
(28)   *NTP 9th Report on Carcinogens*
(29)   *Health Effects of Chemicals Found in Cigarette Smoke* Physicians
         for a Smoke Free Canada: *SECONDHAND SMOKE* September 1999
(30)   Vancouver Smoke-Free By-Law Prosecutions to Date, Vancouver
         City Council, British Columbia. March 2000
(31)   *Indoor Air Quality: Alternative Strategy* Bates Number
         2025858759
(32)   *Nicotine Addiction Is Ruled a Disability in British Columbia:*
         Seattle Pacific University March 8, 2000 *Seattle Times*

VI - TOBACCO AND THE P.R. WAR
Two Sides of the Same Tarnished Coin

(1)   *Ibid* Chapter X (10)
(2)   *Big Talk and Big Tobacco* ABC News John Stossel *Give Me A
        Break* February 9, 2001
(3)   2000 Annual Election Report *Elections B.C.* page 22
(4)   *The Nation: George W. Bush Calling for Philip Morris* November
        8, 1999
(5)   *Ibid*
(6)   *4H- YES! Philip Morris – NO!* The Onyx Group, August 30, 2000
(7)   *Tobacco's Dirty Tricks* Americans for Nonsmokers Rights
(8)   *Astro Turf: Bogus Grass Roots Group and the Tobacco Industry,
        Pacific Sun, Marin County* March 13 – 19, 1996
(9)   *Americans for Nonsmokers' Rights: The Oakridge National
        Laboratory (ORNL) Links to the Tobacco* Industry February 10,
        2000 : Tobacco *Money Lights Up a Debate: Science* 272: 488-
        494; April 26, 1996
(10)   June 12, 1987 letter Bates 508220698
(11)   *New Civilization News: HealthNet Daily: A Different Kind of
        Doctor's Group* December 9, 2000
(12)   *Tobacco's Toll: Implications for the Pediatrics (RE4001):* Ameri-
        can Academy of Pediatrics Policy Statement Volume 107, Number
        4, April 2001. Pp794-798
(13)   American Academy of Pediatrics *History/Mission Statement/
        Structure and Governance* 2001
(14)   *Philip Morris and the Hospitality Industry: Our Mission: To
        maintain the Ability for Our Consumers to Enjoy Our Products in
        Public Venues*: Bates Number 2045517337/2045517347
(15)   Non-Smokers' Rights Association/Smoking and Health Action Foun-

dation: *Tobacco Industry Front Groups in Canada* April 27, 2000

(16) *New York Times: Lobby Admits to Higher Spending in Smoking-Law Fight*, Clifford J. Levy December 12, 1998

(17) *PR Watch: Vol 3 No. 3: Wolves in Sheep's Clothing: "Special Interest Watchdogs" Exposed as Tobacco Industry Front Group* John Stauber and Sheldon Rampton

(18) *Ibid*

(19) *California Initiative* Internal Memorandum to G. Bible from E. Merlo January 12, 1994 Bates 2022839335

(20) *Journal of the American Medical Association: Tourism and Hotel Revenues Before and After Passage of Restaurant Smoke-Free Ordinances,* Stanton A. Glantz, Ph.D., Annemarie Charlesworth, M.A. Volume 281 No. 20. May 26, 1999.

(21) *Ibid* Chapter III (1)

(22) *Reputation Management: Case Study: Tobacco Institute: Farewell to the Tobacco Institute, PR At Its Worst* Selz/Seabolt Communications July 31, 1997

(23) *Ibid*

(24) *Ibid*

(25) *Public Smoking: The Problem*: Tobacco Institute speech, 1985. TIMN0014554/4565

(26) *Ibid*

(27) *Ibid*

(28) Tobacco Institute memorandum discussing the repercussions of the word "addicted" being added to cigarette package information. September 9, 1980. TIMN Number 0107822/7823

(29) *Antismoking Practices of the Insurance Industry:* Tobacco Institute internal memorandum November 22, 1989. TIFL 0543635/3636

(30) *Ibid*

(31) *Ibid* Chapter III (30)

(32) *Ibid*

(33) *"Asia ETS Project Consultant Status Report" Privileged and Confidential Attorney's Work Project* February 14, 1990 Bates Number 2500048976-98

(34) *The Cigarette Papers: Smoking Guns: Industry Asia Plan on ETS. South China Morning Post* January 18, 1999. Hedley Thomas and Jason Gagliardi

(35) *Ibid* (31)

(36) *Ibid* (22)

(37) *Public Finance Balance of Smoking in the Czech Republic* Arthur D. Little International, Inc. researched prepared for Philip Morris November 28, 2000

(38) *Ibid*

(39)   *Ibid*
(40)   *Philip Morris Plan: "More Death, Less Taxes"* Ellen Goodman,
        Boston Globe July 19, 2001
(41)   Vancouver Board of Trade Media Release: Fireworks Festival Society:
        Public/Private Partnership Saves Summer Fireworks May 31, 2001

VII - THE BEGINNING OF THE END
Smoking Restrictions and First Legal Victories Against Tobacco

(1)   *Tobacco Information and Prevention Source ("TIPS"):* National
        Center for Chronic Disease Prevention and Health Promotion
        (CDC) November 2, 2000
(2)   *Ibid*
(3)   Facts on File: World News CDROM June 26, 1997
(4)   *Public Citizen: Discovery Abuse: How Defendants in Products
        Liability Lawsuits Hide and Destroy Evidence"*, page 18 David
        Halperin, Congress Watch. July 1997
(5)   CNN U.S. NEWS: *Secondhand Smoke Deal Creates Research
        Foundation.* October 10, 1997
(6)   CNN-U.S. News. *"Settlement Reached in Minnesota Tobacco
        Case"* May 8, 1998
(7)   COURT TV Trials: *"Battling the Odds"* Bryan Robinson. August
        27, 1998

VIII - MILLIONS FOR BILLIONS
Millions Die From Tobacco Use for Unlimited Profits

(1)   *Ibid* Chapter VII (1)
(2)   *PBS "The American Experience – The Guerrilla War"* WGBH
(3)   *Smoking-Attributable Mortality and Years of Potential Life Lost –
        United States, 1990* Centres for Disease Control and Prevention, *Mor-
        bidity and Mortality Weekly Report 1993; 42 (33):645-9*
(4)   *Ibid* (1)
(5)   *Ibid* Chapter I (5)
(6)   Mayo Clinic, Rochester: Pulmonary and Critical Care Medicine Divi-
        sion, Department of Internal Medicine: *Lung Cancer* January 12, 2000
(7)   *New Screening Test Offers Hope in Lung Cancer Detection: Health
        Matters* Dr. Eric Perlman, The Medical Center at Princeton. No-
        vember 21, 1999.
(8)   *The Health Consequences of Smoking* McGill Medical Faculty,
        McGill University. Molson Informatics Project supervised by Dr.
        Michael Rosengarten, Professor of Medicine, McGill University.
(9)   *Estimates of Smoking-Attributable Deaths at Ages 15-54, Mother-*

less or Fatherless Youths, and Resulting Social Security Costs in the United States in 1994: Preventive Medicine 30; 353-360 (2000) Bruce N. Leistikow, M.D., M.S.; Daniel C. Martin, B.S.; Christina B. Milano, B.A.

(10)   *Ibid (8)*

(11)   *Ibid*

(12)   *Ibid*

(13)   *Ibid*

(14)   *Ibid*

(15)   *Ibid*

(16)   *Ibid* (5)

(17)   *Ibid* (15)

(18)   *Ibid*

(19)   *Ibid*

(20)   *Ibid*

(21)   *Ibid*

(22)   *Ibid*

(23)   *Smoking and Pregnancy*, Moner. The Canadian Task Force on the Periodic Health Examination. Clinical Preventive Health Care. Ottawa: Canada Communication Group – Publishing, 1994: 26-36

(24)   *Osteoporosis and Bone Densitomitry: Does the Emperor Have Clothes? Canadian Medical Association Journal* , Brian C. Lentle, M.D. November 17, 1998

(25)   *Clean and Sober But Dying for a Smoke. Connecticut Association of Addiction Professionals* , Robert H. Shipley, Ph.D., *CAAP Connection* April 1999

(26)   *Alcohol Alert: National Institute on Alcohol Abuse and Alcoholism* No. 39 page 1 *The Co-Occurrence of Alcoholism and Smoking*

(27)   *Puffed Up Egos: Inhaling in Distress* Barbara Beckwith. Harvard School of Medicine *Harvard Magazine* March-April 2001 Volume 104. No. 4. Page 14

(28)   *Smoking Linked to Loss of Vision: Journal of the American Medical Association* Johanna M. Seddon, M.D. October 9, 1996

(29)   *Tobacco Reference Link; chapter 38:* David Moyer, M.D., Associate Clinical Professor of Medicine, University of California

(30)   *Physicians for a Smoke Free Canada*

(31)   *Researchers Show How Smoking Causes Cancer: The Wall Street Journal* Jerry E. Bishop and Milo Geyelin, October 18, 1996

(32)   World Health Organization South East Asia Region: *Tobacco Industry Strategies to Lure Women*

(33)   *Heart Disease and Women: Kicking the Smoking Habit.* National Institutes of Health: National Heart, Lung and Blood Institute Publication Number 94-3657 August 1995 page 1

(34)   *An Overview of the Known Health Effects of Smoking During Preg-
         nancy:* Dr. Sandra Hacker, Federal Vice-President, American Medi-
         cal Association

(35)   *Ibid*

(36)   *Ibid*

(37)   *Carcinogen in Tobacco Smoke Can Be Passed to Fetus: British Medi-
         cal Journal* August 29, 1998; 317:555. Jacqui Wise, BMJ

(38)   *Facts About Heart Disease and Women: Are You At Risk?* National
         Heart, Lung and Blood Institute, National Institute of Health, U.S.
         Dept. of Health and Human Services Public Health Service NIH Pub-
         lication No. 98-3654 1995

(39)   *Maternal Cigarette Smoking and Oral Clefts: A Meta-Analysis: Cleft
         Palate-Craniofacial Journal* May 1997 Vol. 34, No. 3; Diego F.
         Wyszynski, M.D., M.H.S., Ph.D.; David L. Duffy, M.B.B.S., Ph.D.;
         Terri H. Beaty, Ph.D.

(40)   *Trends in Lung Cancer Mortality Among Men and Women, Wisconsin
         and the United States, 1979 – 1994: Wisconsin Medical Journal.* No-
         vember 1997, Jennifer L. Kujak, M.S.; Patrick Remington, M.D., M.P.H.

(41)   *Tobacco – Health Facts: World Health Organization* Fact Sheet 221
         April 1999

(42)   *Risk of Tobacco Sickness: Journal of the American Medical Asso-
         ciation.* Rebecca Voelker. Vol 283 No. 12. March 22/29, 2000

(43)   *Ibid* (30)

(44)   *Ibid*

(45)   *Ibid*

(46)   *Ibid*

(47)   *Ibid*

(48)   *Ibid*

(49)   *Ibid*

(50)   *Ibid*

(51)   *American Council for Drug Education: Basic Facts About Drugs:
         Tobacco*

(52)   *Profits Per Cigarette, 1990 – 2000: Physicians for a Smoke-Free
         Canada* March 2001: Annual Reports Imasco 1990 – 1998, Imperial
         Tobacco 1999 – 2000

(53)   *Tobacco Information and Prevention Source: National Center for
         Chronic Disease Prevention and Health Promotion* November 2, 2000

IX - CIGARETTE LIGHTER SIDE
Mouth Fires and Comical Tobacco Liars

(1)   *Ibid* Dedication (2)

(2)   *Ibid* Dedication (1)

(3)   *R. J. Reynolds Chief: Smoking Isn't Addicting: CNN U.S. News 'Tobacco Under Attack'* August 13, 1997

(4)   *The WorldPaper: The Truth About Lies: Addicted to Tobacco Industry's Big Lie.* March, 1998. Brad Durham/Global Investor Publishing, Inc.

(5)   *Industry Exec: Tobacco No Worse Than Tomato Juice: CNN U.S. News 'Tobacco Under Attack'* August 19, 1997

(6)   *Tobacco Industry Quotes: A Sample; Americans for Nonsmokers' Rights*

(7)   *Things Said in Seriousness: Brooke Shields*

(8)   Mark Twain

(9)   Anon.

(10)   Anon.

(11)   The Quitsmoking Co., 3675 Glenvale Court, Cumming, GA 30041 Phone 1-770-346-9222; FAX: 1-770-4755007.
        Web site: http://www.quitsmoking.com/contactus.htm

X - TOBACCO: PLAGUE OF THE NEW MILLENIUM
The Momentum Builds for a Smoke-Free World

(1)   Towards a Tobacco-Free California:Strategies for the 21st Century 2000-2003, Tobacco Education and Research Oversight Committee, 1999 page 11

(2)   *Ibid*

(3)   *Ibid*

(4)   *B.C. Leading the Pack on Tobacco*; Heart & Stroke Foundation of B.C. & the Yukon; Canadian Cancer Society B.C. & Yukon Division; B.C. Lung Association; 1996 edition, page 25

(5)   *Hannibal Courier-Post* June 30, 2001 *Quit Cigarettes and Become a Millionaire*, Jim Davidson

(6)   The Guardian May 16, 2001 EU *Go-Ahead for Grim Pictures on Cigarette Packs*

(7)   ACSH: Letter from Peter Brosnan to Dr. Whelan June 23, 2001

(8)   Nicotine Anonymous World Services, 419 Main Street, PMB #370, Untington Beach, California 92648

(9)   American Lung Association, *What are the Benefits of Quitting Smoking*? July 30, 2001

EPILOGUE & BOYCOTT LIST

(1)   By kind permission of Gene Borio, Tobacco News Daily, funded by the Robert Wood Johnson

(2)   Conscientious Consuming: The Boycott Against Tobacco Companies

• INDEX •

A

Addiction, nicotine 37, 44, 50, 87, 90, 97, 106, 125, 130, 133, 171
   Dopamine 53, 91
   Cigarettes more addictive than heroin 133
   pH levels in spit tobacco adjusted for youth absorption 38-39
   Ruled a disability in B.C. court 119
   SPECT/PET brain scans 91
   Tobacco industry research about: five year olds 40, 44

Advertising, tobacco   False claims: asbestos filters 24, 93-96
                            More Doctors Recommend 17-22, 31

Alcoholics: more die from tobacco than alcohol 149

American Academy of Pediatrics (AAP) 125

Ammonia chemistry: Marlboro cigarettes leading sales brand
                            maximize nicotine 'hit' to the brain, impact
                            booster, freebase nicotine 90

Association of American Physicians and Surgeons (AAPS) support tobacco 125

B

Baker, Dr. Ray foreword, 67

Bass, Dr. Fred 67

Bans, smoking, cut Philip Morris profits by $40 million in one year 127

"Business Edge" Benson & Hedges promotion of cigarette vending machines 126

C

Cato Institute: funded by tobacco 82, 87
                            *Lies, Damned Lies and 40,000 Smoking
                            Related Deaths* 82

Child Abuse: exposure of children to secondhand smoke
                            is child abuse 110

China   tobacco market 99
                            free cigarettes in discos 101
                            sponsorship Beijing radio 101
                            "Marlboro American Music Hour" 101

Colby, Frank G., RJR Manager/Director 80

Collishaw, Neil, Physicians for a Smoke-Free Canada 67, 81, 86

Coumarin: lung specific carcinogen added to pipe
                            tobacco Project Coumarin 51, 92

"Courtesy of Choice"   tobacco campaign for Canadian tobacco
                            front groups 117

Czechoslovakia: Philip Morris Report claiming early death of
                            smokers good for economy 134

LECTURES, WORKSHOPS, KEYNOTES: Presentations to all ages from elementary & high school to parents' groups, educators, tobacco intervention and prevention seminars and conferences.

VISIT OUR WEBSITE FOR UPDATED INFORMATION:
www.you-are-the-target.com

ORDER MORE COPIES:

**CAN $18.50 US $16.90 plus applicable taxes and shipping
Visa & Mastercard accepted**

Contact:

**Chryan Communications
Vancouver, British Columbia, Canada**

**Phone: (604) 740-3883
Fax: (604) 740-3884**

Email: chryancomm@dccnet.com